MENTAL DETOX

The Power and Guidance to Implement
Peace, Joy, Balance and Financial
Abundance in Your Life

Cheyenne Bryant

First Printing: 2014

Cover design: Book Baby

www.mentaldetoxbook.com

Printed in the United States of America

ISBN 978-0-578-15180-9

Acknowledgements:

My Amazing Parents: Maria Ortega;

John Bailey James;

Kim Ortega; Darren Bryant

My Loved Ones: Ronnika Barnes; Joshua Brandon; Louis Brandon; Natalie Brandon; Aaliyah Bryant; Dior Bryant; Kharisma Bryant; Marco Carr; Gina Clayton; Ruth Clayton; Michelle Garcia; John Gordon; Michael Gray; Ebony Hayes; April James; Lydia King; Lil Louie; Akia Madden; Connie Meriwether; Jemishawa Meriwether; Latrice Northern; Momma Ola; Adrian Ortega; Adriana Ortega; Chayne Ortega; Chermaine Ortega; Louis Ortega; Melody Peterson; Triston Northern-Tyler; Tammy Upshaw; Iyanla Vanzant; Tiffani Walker; Maxine Wheeler; Shavon Williams; Wesley Williams III; Marianne Williamson; Vanity Woods; Lola Yates.

"You are a rose placed in my garden. All the beauty!"

– Auntie April

TABLE OF CONTENTS

Introduction

In today's ever-advancing landscape of technological ingenuity, increased opportunities and seemingly endless resources, we find ourselves in the middle of a strange paradox. We have created nano robots that can perform intricate surgeries, drones that can carry out remote control wars, and genetically engineered crops, but despite these miraculous feats, we still struggle with the most primal emotions of fear, loneliness, anger and deep sadness. The human race still hasn't figured out how to make peace, love and compassion our most precious priorities, and as a result, the walking wounded abound.

The good news is that the desire to heal, change and grow is the hallmark of every living thing on this planet. Each system, whether plant, animal or human, seeks balance and will strive to achieve wholeness and optimal health. However, there are times when our wounds are too great to heal on our own and we must turn to others for assistance. That is where working with a trained and highly-skilled life coach or psychotherapist can be invaluable. A trusted ally and guide on your healing journey can mean the difference between spending years in turmoil, reinventing the wheel, or being free to use that time to create the life of your dreams. As someone who has embarked upon this journey myself and has come out the other side infinitely stronger and wiser, my chief passion in life is to assist others with their personal and god-chosen transformation. I believe that everything happens for a reason, and today I am grateful for every event and experience in my past, because it has brought me here to be of service to you, the reader. I look forward to planting positive seeds in all individuals that I come in contact with.

This book is written for anyone that has a genuine desire to heal and grow, and the courage to stretch themselves beyond self-limitations. Those who have the willingness to implement peace, joy, balance and financial abundance in their lives will find the hope and support in this book that they need to make the leap. Although it is ideal to work with a life coach in person on a regular basis, it is not always feasible due to various personal constraints, including location, health and work schedule, so it is my hope that this book can also offer a lifeline to these individuals between sessions.

My approach is based on several core beliefs. The first is that we create our own circumstances. I believe in the Law of Attraction, and I believe that everything is learned behavior – therefore we can unlearn anything that is not serving our highest purpose. In short, we are more powerful than we can ever imagine! We can learn to cultivate our lives like a garden, choosing what to plant and grow, and what to remove. Although we may have suffered greatly as children, we are no longer victims of the past. Today we can move beyond mere survival, and embrace our ability to thrive. I'm not religious, but I am spiritual. I do not believe in bad or good; I believe things just *are*. I don't believe any one individual is inferior or superior to another, as we all are on our OWN journey and are perfect just as we are. I feel it is important for people to stand in their authentic self and personal power, because their true essence in its rawest form is *love*. Love is the most powerful force that heals and balances all. This is why people are PERFECT just as they are!

As I mentioned, I myself embarked on a similar journey as the one you are undertaking, and that is what led to my desire to become a Doctor of Psychology and a Spiritual Life Coach. I attended Cal State University of Northridge at the age of 17. While there, I obtained a double degree in Psychology and Pan African studies. For my first two years, I was undecided as to what field I should pursue as a career. Organically, I ended up choosing psychology. I still wasn't quite sure why, however. I didn't realize what had triggered my interest until I entered the Master's Program at University of Phoenix. I was about halfway through my Master's and boom! It hit me! I had A LOT of healing that needed to be done. My desire for self-fulfillment, healing, peace, and balance within myself drew me to the field of psychology. It wasn't until I began healing others, that I began to heal myself. You see, healing is transparent. God works through transparency. What God moves through you, he gives to you!

I remember working as a psychotherapist intern and receiving a client that had experienced sexual abuse at a very intense level. There were times when the client would weep while telling me the many stories of her rape experiences. I would ask permission to support her by placing my hand on her back or shoulder, and she would tense up and reply, "No, please don't touch me."

During one session, this client began to describe how she felt after the sexual abuse –dirty, embarrassed, victimized, shamed, guilty, disgusted, and violated. I found myself chiming in and taking the words right out of her mouth. The session with this young lady triggered emotions in me regarding my own sexual abuse experience. I quickly checked my emotions and allowed her to finish expressing herself. By that time, she had figured out that I too had experienced similar circumstances. From that point on there was an unspoken connection between the client and I.

Following the session, I checked in with my supervisor and therapist colleagues. I explained the triggers and countertransference I felt during the session and shared my sexual abuse story with them. My supervisor asked if I wanted to transfer the client to another therapist and I said, "No, I can handle it." God makes no mistakes! I believe that God assigns people to each other to enable their growth. There is NO such thing as a coincidence. That client and I were assigned to one another to heal, as we both needed healing in the same area. It was a clear example of the Law of Attraction in action. And we did just that; we healed simultaneously.

At the end of one of the sessions toward the end of treatment, the client turned to me and said, "I'm ready for a hug now." I literally had to hold back my tears. I too was able to make huge leaps forward in my healing. After 16 years of keeping my experience from my family, I was able to sit down with them and release that pain. My client healed with the help of my skill, training, and effective treatment, and I healed in the midst of assisting her.

That was my first "aha" moment. I understood that no one heals alone, and that healing is transparent and reciprocal. That intensified my desire to serve God and people at all levels. I understood that my life is my ministry and that all of my adversities, tribulations, and circumstances were obtained to assist and guide others through similar journeys. My soul-searching had just begun. I began to meditate daily and research spirituality.

During my spiritual journey, I ran across a book written by a good friend of mine, Tyrese Gibson, *How to Get Out Of Your Own Way*. I started reading this book as soon as I boarded the plane from LAX to Miami and I couldn't tear my eyes away from the page. I remember every so often turning to my fiancé at that time and saying, "OMG, babe! This book complements my thinking exactly!" This book intensified my desire for spiritual growth even more. By time we landed, I had completed the book and had purchased another book on my Kindle. It was the book Tyrese mentioned had inspired him to write his own story, *As a Man Thinketh* by James Allen. I read that book in our hotel room while my fiancé got dressed. He was on vacation, but I was starving for more spiritual feeding!

Once we returned home, I was watching Iyanla Vanzant's show, "Iyanla Fix My Life," on the OWN network. Boy was that a mistake! The phrase, "Stay in PEACE not pieces," stuck to me like a child on their first day of pre-school! I studied that woman with an eagle's eye. I screamed at the TV, sat on the edge of the couch, and rewound the show (which I had recorded) at least 30 times. By the end of the night, I had ordered her book on my Kindle, *Peace From Broken Pieces*. I fell in love with her honest, down to earth, warm spirit. By the end of the week I had googled and researched her and learned that she facilitated healing retreats. I was registered for that retreat, flight booked, and ready to go the next day!

The retreat was for five days in Rhinebeck, New York. Now mind you, I had never traveled alone, and definitely had never slept alone in the suburbs or in the woods, as I'm a city girl to my core. The retreat was titled, "The Law of Cause and Effect" and was held at the Omega Institute for Holistic Studies in Rhinebeck, a breathtaking spiritual center. I wish I could go into detail and provide words that would describe the depth of healing and the ebb and flow of energy that took place there, but to define a thing is to limit it. I will just say that the healing, awareness, and spiritual growth that took place at this retreat was indescribable and limitless! Put it this way: I cried from the moment I walked in, down to the second I boarded my flight to return home. Did I forget to mention that I returned to her "Wonder Woman Weekend" retreat in Maryland 8 months later? Well, I did! And that retreat enhanced my spiritual growth and intensified my hunger to heal and heal others at a higher level of consciousness.

Today, I work at my own private practice, helping individuals, couples and groups of all backgrounds and ages. I attend Circle of Wealth power brunches and power gatherings to connect and network with my peers, exchange ideas and foster abundance. I also share my experiences via speaking engagements and on the lecturing circuit. I am always evolving, constantly seeking out new ways to be of service to my clients and effect positive change in their lives. *Mental Detox* is a summary of all that I have learned and absorbed on my path, but although the book stands alone as a completed work, my life is an endless work in progress.

In order to create an accessible and enjoyable roadmap for the reader, this book is organized around the central image of a garden. A garden is a place where creativity, responsibility, dedication and hard work converge to produce an environment of beauty and tranquility. The garden is a metaphor for your life, and each chapter explores a different aspect of the work you must do to transform it into your own sacred, sustainable sanctuary. Negative thoughts, self-defeating patterns, damaged relationships and limiting emotions are the weeds that must be rooted out if you are to plant positive seeds for the future. As you navigate each topic and begin to delve deeper into your consciousness, remember to always be gentle. Handle yourself each day as you would a precious orchid, for you are a child of God and a great treasure!

With the help of this book, you will learn to stand in your own power, and know your own authentic voice, no matter how long it has been suppressed. You will know health on all levels – physical, mental and spiritual. You will learn new, dynamic coping skills to replace the ones that cause you damage and pain. Your entire state of being will be altered, and you will no longer resist all the good that life has in store for you. Your relationships will blossom, for you will now know your true value and you will cease to dishonor yourself with those who do not acknowledge your boundless light. In your career and work life, you will experience exponential growth. But rather than describing yourself as a list of achievements, you will be able to own and celebrate everything about yourself, even your so-called flaws. Financial abundance will overflow from your cup, for once you discover your internal wealth, external wealth will follow and you will prosper effortlessly. Joy, self-awareness and enlightenment will flow throughout your life as naturally as your breath, and you will want nothing more than to share the gifts of your healing process with the world. You will no longer wish to hide your talents in the shadows, and stripped of all guilt, shame and fear, you will know true prosperity. You will be whole.

Change comes at a price, however. Do not be surprised if you experience resistance, both from yourself and from others. Resistance is normal. It means you're doing something right! Where the resistance is the growth is. Sometimes that resistance will manifest as physical symptoms. You might contract an inexplicable headache right when you are about to make a major breakthrough at work. Or you might find your stomach upset right before you are scheduled to have a talk with your romantic partner about moving forward. Don't give up! Every time you forge ahead despite obstacles, the obstacles lose their power to detain you from your goals. Other times resistance comes in the form of friends and family who don't want you to change. They may prefer the old you, the one who they are comfortable with, even if that person isn't the real you. Change is threatening to a lot of people because it reminds them of what they might be avoiding themselves, and by evolving, you also challenge them to evolve. If they're not ready to do that, they may try to dissuade or distract you from your inner work. They may even judge or reject you. Don't let this deter you. Simply offer up a prayer for every person in your life to find happiness and the strength to face their troubles head on. Prayer can be empowering in such situations, where resentment would only poison the positive mental environment you are striving to build. So prepare yourself! Prepare to be stretched. Prepare to experience fear and to overcome it. Prepare to be used by the Universe and God to enlighten and inspire others. Prepare yourself to be uncomfortable, for you are about give birth to a brand new you!

In addition to being gentle with yourself at all times on this journey, try to set aside time for yourself each day to just be alone and reflect on what you are reading and how it makes you feel. There is no need to rush through the book. It is not going anywhere! I also highly recommend beginning counseling with a trained therapist or life coach if you have not already done so. It's important to seek out support beyond just reading books. If something comes up while you are reading and you're all alone with it, you can become re-traumatized rather than reaching the epiphany or catharsis that a compassionate and experienced guide can facilitate. If you wish to make an appointment with me, you can always contact me at DrBryant@DrBryant.co. With a loving co-traveler in your corner, there is no circumstance that you cannot overcome and no pain so great that it cannot be lessened!

Chapter 1: The Garden of Life

"The soul never thinks without an image." – Aristotle

Our ability to call forth powerful mental pictures that affect our health, our thinking, our feelings and our circumstances, is a uniquely human capacity. No other animal is able to harness such a stunning and reality-altering skill. Combining abstract thought with words and pictures, we have built a world limited only by our imaginations. Every building, spaceship, government, screenplay, restaurant, baseball field or ballroom gown was first conceived as a blueprint in the mind of man, for we are primarily creative beings. This creativity is our birthright, and it is the key to personal growth and change. We are like artists painting a grand tableau. We have the power to revise, improve, or completely reinvent the canvas at any moment in time using the mind's unlimited potential for personal transformation.

Guided imagery and healing visualization has been formally used in psychotherapy since the 1960's, but the use of imagery goes back centuries. The Eye of Horus was a symbol used in Egypt to denote good health, protection from harm and prosperity. Shamans used the Sun Spiral as a symbol of universal healing, representing the benevolent light that radiates from above. And we are all familiar with the Asclepius Wand, a symbol often seen in the medical field, which comes from a Bible story. Moses was told to construct a serpent-adorned brass pole that would heal all those who gazed upon it. These ancient cultures all acknowledged that we could draw strength from ideas, and use these positive images as a kind of mental medicine.

In this book, I invite you to use the mental image of a garden on your healing journey. This garden represents your life. It has many components, including your mind, your heart, your body, your soul, your work life and your romantic life, but all these areas are under your control as the Master Gardener. This garden can either become your oasis, a sanctuary of peace, prosperity and joy, or it can become a weed-infested wasteland, overrun with unwanted foliage, pests and debris.

When we speak of Mental Detox, we are talking about rooting out all the undesirables from your garden and replacing them with orchids, roses and fruit trees, a clean rushing fountain and immaculate, well-maintained lawns. This means getting rid of negativity in all forms; bad habits such as self-pity, procrastination, gossip, fits of anger, self-defeating patterns of self-sabotage; and the rotting, underground wounds of the past, such as childhood traumas, abuse, neglect and family dysfunction. We then can choose to replace these liabilities with new assets: gratitude, humor, humility, fortitude and authenticity. Mental detox, like gardening, takes hard work and perseverance, but there is no one else who can do the job. It cannot be outsourced to another party. A therapist or life coach can guide you, giving you the right tools and showing you the path, but you are ultimately responsible for your life.

Our lives, like our bodies, follow the rules of homeostasis. If there is imbalance, stress or tension, our system will strive to heal itself. This means that we can either consciously choose to move forward and face our difficulties, surrendering to the process with grace, or we can be dragged. If we choose denial, we may be forced to change by negative circumstances and experiences along the lines of a "wake-up call." This might be a DUI, the loss of a marriage, getting fired, or becoming inexplicably ill. These are manifestations of our inner blockage played out in the physical world. When our dysfunction reaches this point, it's much more difficult to ignore than emotional pain such as depression or anxiety. We now have very concrete penalties for neglecting our gardens. We may think of these misfortunes as "happening to us," and lament our bad luck, but upon closer inspection we will find that we played a part in their unfolding, either by ignoring important warnings from our bodies, our partners or our bosses, or by refusing to grow or move forward. Growth is inevitable, for life never stands still. To stand still is to stagnate. Every living thing is on a path of maturation, from conception to demise. That is why they call it the wheel of life – it is always turning. When fear causes us to refuse to grow in some way, either professionally or personally, we manifest a host of problems and pain. Eliminate fear and EVERY door will open!

Here is where the Law of Attraction comes into play. The Law of Attraction is based on the idea that like everything else in nature, our thoughts have energy. Thoughts are a very light and fast form of energy that can be easily transformed and manipulated, whereas a submarine, for instance, would be a very heavy, slow form of energy that is not easily converted to another form. Because our thoughts are so light and fast, we tend to dismiss them, without realizing how powerful they can be. But as I mentioned before, every man-made structure, relationship or job began as a simple thought. The energy moved from lightness to heaviness, from imagination to existence.

Thoughts are vibrations that broadcast an audible signal into the universe, much like radio waves. Our bodies pick up on them, as do other people. A good example might be when you walk into a room and "sense" tension between a group of people. No words may have been spoken, but you can 'hear' the negative energy and it may set you on edge. Thought waves of energy are like nets we cast out, and they bring back exactly what we envision. *You bring about what you think about.* If we are devoting great mental energy to picturing our worst fears – failure, illness, isolation and pain – we tend to attract these types of situations to us, because we are constantly focusing on them.

You can also think of this in more physical terms. Let's say your thoughts are people. Imagine these thoughts are dressed in grungy clothes. These thoughts have not shaved in weeks, and they smell bad. When these thoughts go out into a public space, who will they attract? Not the healthy, happy people on their way to work. No, these grungy thoughts will attract their own kind. Now, let's say your thoughts are full of positive energy, light and love. These thoughts will attract positivity into your life, for they will be recognized and embraced as fellows by positive people, places and situations. Like attracts like, just as birds of a feather will flock together.

The Law of Attraction is not about trying to completely avoid unpleasant life events. Rather, it is about cultivating a perception that interprets challenging events as opportunities rather than misfortunes. The Chinese word for 'crisis' or 'problem' is also their word for opportunity. If our minds are focused on positive outcomes, we will experience one, regardless of how things may seem on the surface. A broken leg is seen as a long awaited chance to catch up on personal correspondence and reading; the loss of a 9-5 job is viewed as inspiration to start a business; a failed relationship creates the space for a partner that is even more ideal. Remember that adversity and failure provide a strength that lasts forever. They give us a place to pull strength from that others may never obtain or experience.

Another way to look at the Law of Attraction is to think about a series of experiments involving cats. Researchers Blakemore and Cooper raised two kittens in two different environments. One had horizontal stripes, and one had vertical stripes. What they discovered was that as the kittens grew up, they could not navigate environments that lacked their type of childhood stripes. The kittens' eyes simply weren't able to recognize a different pattern. In our lives, if we experienced anger or cruelty at the hands of our caretakers, this is the only thing we can "see" in the world. We keep repeating those same dysfunctional relationships because we cannot even recognize another possibility. We are like blind cats. But once we open up to the notion that there is a completely different set of 'stripes' out there going the opposite way, we can slowly accept a new reality. We may meet a kind teacher, friend or life coach. Gradually we will begin to see kindness around us. And this perception reinforces our experience. We start to draw kindness like a magnet, because we expect it. Slowly all the hurt and pain is a distant memory. We don't expect it, and we don't fear it. It's just not part of our orientation any more. We are no longer love-blind.

Another image I find very helpful is that of a drum circle. Each good thing you aspire to is like a drum. You want to create a symphony of all your good, by banging over and over on the drums you like. If you meet someone wonderful, you can think of them as a djembe. You want to keep repeating the delightful sound of that drum, by spending more time with this person, deepening your friendship. Let's say you find a hobby you enjoy like surfing. This is your bongo. You start playing your bongo every day, reinforcing that positive feeling of joy. The music spreads, and soon the drum circle grows larger. People come from all over to participate and enjoy your drum circle. They are attracted to you like a magnet. This is prosperity. Your wealth grows as does your circle of friends.

And it all starts with just finding one drum you like to play and playing it over and over. You may be very happy to have all these new friends and opportunities, but this happiness did not originate externally. It came from inside you, from a special joy you found that is yours alone to share with the world. This also shows you that success is for everyone. It is not some limited resource that can only be obtained by a chosen few. The Law of Attraction shows us that when we open up to becoming truly authentic in our desires, emotions and abilities, there is no limit on what we can achieve, because we offer something to the world that is totally unique. Love is the merchandise that all the world demands; if you store it in your heart, every soul will become your customer.

Creating your beautiful, refreshing garden has several phases. Step one is to take stock of your current situation. If you were to visualize your life as a garden right now, what would you see? Are there certain areas in the shadows where you don't dare to go because of the mess? Are there whole sections that you have never explored due to fear of the unknown? Do you see what were once lovely flowering trees now dry and crumbling because you've neglected to water them? Begin to think about what in your life needs attention. Is it your health? Your relationships? Your career? Do you suffer from a perpetually broken heart? Begin to cultivate the willingness to perform honest self-examination.

The second phase of our gardening plan involves facing these unwanted weeds and uprooting them for good. This is the stage where it will appear that the garden is in even more dis-array than before. All kinds of ugly roots and pesky vines will wind up on the grounds as you dig, exfoliate and exhume the rubble of the past. This is the "feeling" stage. All past trauma must be felt before we can move forward. We can no longer brush all the pain under the rug.

Next we will begin to clarify exactly what we want to attract into our garden. This is the stage where we get to use our design skills! It's time to start drawing up your blueprints. I would say the sky is the limit, however, to define a thing is to limit it. So I will say there is no limit. What long lost dreams can we revive? What new ideas can we explore? Only when we are 100% clear in our intentions, can we begin to attract our great-est good. So we have to wade through the grey areas of inde-cision and indifference to truly become passionate about the future. This takes self-searching and honesty, but the process is an adventure worth savoring. Meditation helps us connect to our deepest joy and hope. It gives us the conviction to make the hard choices that will ultimately make us the happiest. I'm sure you've had the everyday experience of coming home at dinner time and scratching your head over what to eat. You begin to imagine a tasty dinner that involves vegetables, shrimp, your favorite sauce and a fantastic dessert. Once you have a men-tal picture of your meal, you go shopping, get the ingredients and prepare it. The hard part is really coming up with this perfect meal, whereas executing your plan is fairly straightfor-ward and easy to accomplish. So it is with everything in life. You first must decide what you want, down to the last detail.

What kind of job do you want? What kind of partner? Where do you want to live? How do you want to feel every day? The more detail you can come up with, the easier it will be to manifest your dreams. Suddenly, without trying very hard, you start to see bits and pieces of your dream unfolding. You reach out and grab them, acknowledging they match with your plans. Sometimes this can be truly uncanny. You may draw a picture of your ideal home and then literally drive by it on your way to work. It might have been there before, but you never saw it until you consciously named your intention.

Finally, there comes a time when we must stop working and begin receiving. Every garden is an interconnected system. Sunlight, water and nutrients come in, and outcome flowers, trees and butterflies. In order to be productive and thriving, we have to accept assistance from the universe. For some people, this can be the most challenging stage of Mental Detox. Allowing ourselves to be loved, to get paid, to reap rewards and accept success can be difficult if all we've ever known is the struggle. We have the idea we need to do it all alone in order for it to 'count.' But no one is an island. A person who cannot receive is as crippled as one who cannot give. Sharing our beautiful garden with others and with the world motivates us to keep striving for bigger and better things. We have to move into cooperative living, exchanging energy and resources with those around us and accepting our interdependence.

By purchasing and reading this book, you have already taken an enormous step towards changing your life. You've shown the willingness to examine your experience in a new light. In the next chapter we will explore the "feeling" stage of Mental Detox. This will require a great deal of self-compassion and inner strength, but just know that you are incredibly brave to even attempt this work at all. As always, I am here rooting for you and wishing you great happiness and freedom. Remember that when you allow yourself to be stretched beyond your comfort zone, that is where you will find the deepest growth and success!

Chapter 2: The Garden of Wounds

"Our wounds are often the openings into the best and most beautiful part of us."
– David Richo

When I begin working with a new client, my first step is to find out where the impairment is coming from. What is hurting them? And why? Where did the imbalance originate? This is kind of like following a trail of breadcrumbs back to the source of the hurt, which usually occurred in childhood or adolescence when our perceptions first formed. Our perceptions are the unique way in which we interpret events and how we view the world in general. It is like wearing glasses. The observations we make as kids and the environment we grow up in are what determine the prescription to our perceptions. This is also where triggers are formed. No two individuals develop the same perceptions or triggers. We are like snowflakes. Therefore each healing process is unique.

Because our society values an intellectual, self-sufficient approach to problem-solving over the intuitive emotional response, I often encounter clients who attempt to heal using their head rather than their heart. This never works, because the intellectualizing is usually part of a complex system of masks (defense mechanisms) whose purpose is to deflect emotional pain. Instead the feelings come out in convoluted, indirect ways, like blow-outs at work, or as physical manifestations like insomnia. We are also a very action-oriented and achievement-oriented society. Just sitting around feeling emotions doesn't seem like much of an accomplishment. You can't get any kind of award or recognition for it, and some folks might call you 'self-indulgent' for even considering such a pastime. But at some point we have to stop running and simply face ourselves. It is a powerful moment, when we stop running.

As a country that spends over 6 billion a year on the military, many of us grow up with a "soldier" mentality, believing that vulnerability and the expression of emotion are signs of weakness. In fact, it is the opposite. The ability to reveal our tender side; to honestly admit our fears, loneliness and confusion as well as our faults; to stand before our fellows as raw and unmasked, are all signs of a strong, supple and flexible ego. Just think about a blade of grass that bends and sways in the wind. It is flexibility, not rigidity that allows it to cope with obstacles. A stiff blade of grass is a dying blade of grass.

Many of us are not even aware that we live our lives in this avoidant fashion, cut off from our feelings, or stuffing them down through compulsive eating, drinking, shopping or sexual activity. There is such thing as an emotional metabolism. If we don't eliminate our emotions by expressing them – crying, journaling, sharing them with a therapist or life coach, sharing them through artwork or music etc. – we get sick, just as if our digestion system were not working properly. Many people are fearful that if they express anger, it will overcome them, so they shove it down. Expressing anger is not a problem when it's appropriate and short-lived. What becomes a problem is when this anger is covering up other deeper more vulnerable emotions such as grief or fear. Then the anger is functioning as a mask, and again, it is hindering a healthy emotional metabolism.

To put it another way, just like a hangover from alcohol, we can have emotional hangovers when pain from the past is not dealt with properly, either because there was just too much of it to handle at the time, or because we never took the time to process it. Residual pain from the past can color even the brightest of present circumstances with a veil of darkness and depression. Sometimes we may not be aware of its origins, instead finding fault with our current partners, our jobs or our appearances. Worse, we may have allowed the past to affect our choices, influencing us to repeat self-defeating patterns. We never acknowledged our domineering mother, so now we recreate her in our boss and suffer in the present the deep frustrations we repressed all those years ago. We never took the time to mourn our father's abandonment, so now we grieve each male lover that leaves us, never stopping to question where this pattern comes from or why we are allowing it into our lives.

The bottom line is that we have to feel in order to heal. I have a slogan: *Feel, Deal and Heal.* Feeling is mandatory. So get out those tissues! We are going to get our hands dirty!

While emotional pain is part of being human and something we all encounter, not all of our suffering is necessary or ennobling. By this I mean that a lot of times we hold onto our hurts because they are familiar and habitual, but in doing so, we are depleting ourselves of vital energy needed for our present and future. So just remember that dredging up this old gunk is serving a greater purpose. It is so that you can make room in your garden to grow new plants. If all your flowerbeds are covered in kudzu weeds, how can you plant any rosebushes? Let go of the old ways that no longer serve you and embrace the new ones that are jumping with joy to be accepted!

Intellectualizing and anger are not the only masks that keep us from accessing and addressing our wounds. There are many others. Even confidence and worldly success can function as a mask. These traits may be attempts to compensate for hidden feelings of low self-worth. Sure, being an over-achiever might be preferable to being a drug addict, but it is still going to result in a life of inner turmoil. Until the internal feelings are in alignment with the external, the person will experience cognitive dissonance.

Being a compulsive rescuer and savior is another mask. It allows us to focus so heavily on other people's problems that we can completely avoid looking at our own. We might even subconsciously choose a service career for the same reason. Often this type of client will be able to answer questions about the whole family – everyone but themselves. When it comes to what they like, feel or think, they draw a blank.

There is also the mask of the clown. This person learned early on that it was easiest to play the fool instead of attempting to be taken seriously. The clown's life may be littered with self-sabotage, for every time they approach a real achievement or plateau, they retreat to avoid threatening their role as an under-achiever. This is particularly painful for gifted children who may have been ridiculed or ostracized for being exceptional. These kids learned that to stick out, even in a good way, was to invite punishment and hurt. So they resign themselves to a more 'ordinary' existence where they never truly shine, all the while feeling the pain of self-abandonment.

While some masks (workaholism, exercise addiction, scholarly achievement) may be more socially acceptable than others (homelessness, obesity, anger problems,) they all work in the same way to inhibit authenticity. The meaning of the word 'authentic' is 'from the author,' enforcing the idea that you are the one writing your life.

Authenticity is the act of being purely you, without any props, excuses or embellishments. It's the key ingredient in healthy relationships and fulfilling careers.

The journey to authenticity is about un-becoming everything that is <u>not</u> you, so you can be who you were meant to be in the first place. It is about complete vulnerability; exposing all of your imperfections just to find out that those imperfect flaws are exactly what make you PERFECT!

This "feeling" stage of Mental Detox is not pretty. In fact, it's downright ugly! And it's meant to be. Think about what it looks like when they tear down a building. There is a lot of chaos on the scene. Bulldozers plowing into concrete and bits of metal, glass and debris flying every which way. As you clean up your garden you can expect nothing less. The walls that are coming down have kept out not only pain; they have also kept out love. When you live inside such a fortress, you have positioned yourself to survive perhaps, but you have also set yourself up to starve. It's a closed system and as such, it's only a matter of time before it completely breaks down.

Have you ever pulled a weed, only to discover that you didn't quite get to the root and now it's growing up again? Well, it's the same with our defense mechanisms. If we really get down to the roots of our wounds, we can eradicate them forever rather than merely tidying up the surface of our lives with a quick fix. So I say, *lean into the pain.* Let it change you. Let it flood your body and really experience it deeply. Trust in the process! The cure for the pain is in the pain! Literally look at yourself in the mirror and tell yourself, "Lean into the pain!" When you find yourself starting to feel uncomfortable, don't reach for the phone, the TV, the game console or for that bag of chips. Instead, make a conscious effort to sit with the feelings, alone. Even if you're driving, pull over, park your car, and just sit there experiencing your emotions. You'll quickly discover that not only is this more satisfying than all the avoidant behaviors, it actually provides faster relief than all those false forms of self-medication.

Most of all, do not fear solitude. It is fantastic that we live in the age of 'connectedness' where the globe has shrunk so much and we can instantly contact anyone at any time, but in this high tech world of social media, smart phones and tablets, we sometimes need to unplug. We need to spend time alone in order to develop our intuition, to develop intimacy with ourselves. Solitude is like the fresh soil we need in which to plant our fruit trees. Even the most beautiful plants will wither if placed in ground that lacks nutrients or is too shallow. Our foundation must be solid if we are to grow this amazing garden, and we get this foundation through the inner strength we cultivate in solitude. Solitude is different from isolation. It is a conscious, empowered choice to spend time healing, rather than an avoidance of others based on fear. After all, if we don't enjoy spending time with ourselves, why would anyone else enjoy it?

As you begin to identify your patterns of distorted thinking, you will move from victimhood to victory. Victimhood can be its own mask. For example, you may have experienced rejection from your parents as a young child. At the time, you really were a victim of neglect, and no little one should have to experience such betrayal from the people who matter the most. But now as an adult, you are no longer helpless. You can choose your family and your friends. You do not have to keep playing out that role. Furthermore, you can turn this curse into a gift. You can use your pain to develop empathy towards others, the kind that you never received. Today you know the value of planting positive seeds in others. You can be the parent you never had, both to your inner child and to your real life children, if you have them. This is the true victory, when you not only overcome your past, but you are able to use it to benefit other people.

All throughout this journey you will come up against the same underlying adversary: fear. Fear is what lies deep down underneath all the other masks we uproot. We are afraid of success, afraid of failure. Afraid to be alone, and afraid to be with others. We are afraid we are not enough, that we are not as good as others. We are afraid we will lose what we have or not get what we need. We are afraid to die and afraid to live. Fear manifests physically, emotionally, mentally and spiritually, clogging our psychic pipes and sabotaging us at every turn. It is the ultimate weed. Nothing good can grow when fear is the fertilizer.

The flip side of fear is love. But love and fear cannot occupy the same space. They are like two streams rushing in different directions. Fear shuts us down, makes our lives smaller, shrinks our world to the size of a pea while telling us it's for our own good. Love, on the other hand, makes our lives bigger and better. It fills us with joy and the courage to follow our dreams. Both love and fear are contagious. So which would you rather come down with? Which would you rather spread? Love is so powerful that it can melt away years of resistance, insecurity and resentment. In a single moment it can vanish a lifetime of sorrows. Love is the lifeblood of your garden!

The Garden of Wounds

After you have truly cleared away the unwanted, dead or diseased debris by identifying your negative patterns, sharing your wounds with a trusted counselor and dissolving the defense mechanisms that keep you from being authentic, it is time to rebuild. In the next chapter we will explore the harvesting of new crops. We will begin to cultivate all those gorgeous blooms that we have so sorely longed for but were never able to experience. Like the phoenix, from the ashes we will rise anew.

Chapter 3: The Fountain

"Chiefly the mold of a man's fortune is in his own hands."
– Francis Bacon

At the center of your garden lies a golden fountain. This fountain represents the flow of positive, empowering thoughts that drive your actions and emotions, and manifest as your outer circumstances. With careful maintenance and irrigation, this fountain can become a crystal clear beacon of beauty and peace that nurtures every component of your life. In order to achieve this harmonious flow, we have to rebuild our thinking from the ground up. We call this process cognitive restructuring.

To begin cognitive restructuring, we must first identify distorted thought patterns. Some of these include all-or-nothing thinking, ("I am a loser with nothing going for me,") catastrophizing, ("This rejection letter is the end of the world,") making gross generalizations, ("I can't do anything right,") and magical thinking ("I will get a job even though I never go on any interviews.") All these types of cognitive distortions have one thing in common: they are false and make us feel terrible! You may believe that all these thoughts are "reality" or "just the way things are," but they are a choice. You are choosing to feel crummy every time you engage in these types of patterns.

So how do we sow new seeds in our minds? There are several methods. The first is to interrupt the pattern of these negative thoughts. Each time we hear ourselves going down that familiar path towards the painful thoughts, we can ask ourselves, "Is this reality or my perception?" Many times we suffer from a disconnect between reality and perception; this creates cognitive dissonance. We want to be detectives to our thoughts and develop a kind of scientific method to root out the lies and deception that we feed ourselves. We need to develop critical thinking skills, which means that we don't take everything we hear as the gospel truth, especially when it's something negative. We also need to develop a voice similar to that of a good lawyer hired to defend us from these awful accusations that our minds keep throwing at us. Let's say your mind is telling you, "You never do anything right!" Ask yourself, "What evidence you have to support this statement?" Here you can do an exercise such as making a list of all the things you *have* done right, and then a list of some of your mistakes. What you will find is that like all human beings, we are neither perfect nor completely flawed. Each of us excels in some areas while requiring more work in others.

Perhaps you are experiencing an anxiety attack because your mind is telling you, "You're in so much trouble! You are behind at work and you're going to miss the deadline!" Here you can respond by asking yourself three important questions.

"What is the worst case scenario?" Then you can ask, "What is the best case scenario?" And finally, "What is the most realistic scenario?" Perhaps your greatest fear is that you will be fired, and your greatest hope is that no one will notice you're late. But the most realistic scenario is probably one where you have a talk with your boss or client and they get to express their frustrations while you get to offer an explanation. In this way, you can dial down your anxiety by arriving at a middle ground. You can also use this method to make yourself laugh by picturing the most extreme version of your worst case scenario, like your boss throwing a bucket of water on your head. Suddenly the whole problem doesn't seem quite as life-threatening and you can get some perspective. Humor, in fact, is one of the best mood-altering drugs on the planet! It can actually elevate the serotonin levels in your brain, and it does so a lot faster than anti-depressants, drugs or alcohol. Our world with all its sorrow is sorely in need of some chuckles, so remember that as someone that takes the time to make others laugh or bring a smile to their faces, you are making a huge difference.

Some other ways you can change your thoughts and improve your mood are by exercising, listening to uplifting music, meditating and reciting positive affirmations into a mirror. Although I will speak about exercise in another chapter, just know that getting up and walking, getting your blood circulating and your lungs pumping can do wonders for your feelings. A brisk 20-minute walk can literally transform a difficult situation into one with a clear solution.

Music is also a powerful way to get inspired and connect with beauty and tranquility. You can use soothing music to calm down when you are upset, or you can use it to wake up in the morning and get in the groove of taking action towards your new life. As with all media that we consume, from movies to video games, the message matters. This isn't to condone censorship in any form, but if you are trying to build healthy self-esteem and support yourself in becoming more positive and productive, it's best to stay away from media that enforces violence or puts down a certain group of people. A clean happy environment is vital to your mental clarity so make sure that you are setting high standards for what you watch, listen to, or read.

Meditation is a practice that can aid you during every step of your journey. It is as integral to our success as sleeping and eating. Meditation is a chance to calm the mind, to purify the thoughts, and to visualize your highest good. You can begin with just five minutes, focusing on your breathing and becoming fully present. Even with this small amount, you will see vast improvements in your coping skills.

I also highly endorse the use of positive affirmations. I often have my clients gaze into a mirror and first begin naming all the attributes that they do not honor in themselves, verbalizing all that is broken. Next, I instruct them to begin healing these distortions by making kind, compassionate statements towards themselves such as, "I love you," "You are beautiful," or "You are a success." For some, this brings up so much resistance and pain, they can hardly finish the exercise. That is normal. It's all part of Mental Detox! One day you will look into that mirror and really believe those positive statements with all your heart, no matter how far-fetched they may seem in the beginning. (If you don't have a mirror handy, you might try making a list of the unkind things your mind tells you, and then underneath each sentence, write an opposite affirmation.) Because many of us received negative brainwashing as kids in the form of criticism, blaming or belittling, we have to actively brainwash ourselves in the opposite direction! Listening to affirmations on CD can be very helpful, or you can record your own and listen to them at bedtime. You can walk around listening to them in your headphones, and no one will know it's not music. Whatever it takes, you must go to any lengths to root out those nasty, cruel voices and replace them with loving words. Only then will you experience the kind of peace you seek.

Remember that language itself has tremendous power. Every thought and word creates its own reality. If you feel out of control or victimized by current situations, consider reframing your experience by using different words. For instance, you might often say, "I don't have time to date cause I'm too busy with work and school." This perpetuates a sense of lack and deprivation. Instead you can say, "I am choosing to focus on my career right now." It's a much more positive statement, and it probably better reflects your truth, since you could easily choose to make dating a priority by cutting back your hours or postponing school. One type of language breeds helplessness while the other is empowering.

So far we have been speaking about mostly internal means of building self-worth. But there are also external actions we can take to bolster our confidence. By performing esteemable acts where we practice integrity, fairness and patience, we increase our own self-esteem. This means helping and respecting others even if we don't get credit for it. It means choosing to do the right thing, especially when no one is watching. If you are being dishonest, cheating or stealing, or manipulating others in any way, these actions have internal consequences, even if you get away with them. If there is a disconnect between what you consider to be your core values and your outer behaviors, this rift in your integrity will surface as low self-esteem. We often think about our behavior from a perspective of morality, but it's not just about that. If you do something that is unethical in some way, it will erode your ability to focus on your success and create a joyful life of freedom. Imprisonment does not only appear in the form of bars! It also appears in the form of mental imprisonment that is self-inflicted. Do not inflect self-imprisonment by engaging in negative activities! You will only harvest hateful, resentful, fearful, distorted thoughts, and a world of bitterness both within and without. Nothing good can grow in that type of environment. Detox yourself from all forms of fear. After all, lying, stealing or cheating are the ultimately manifestations of fear, and we want to focus exclusively on love. To repeat what I've said earlier, we reap what we sow. If we want to manifest trustworthy friends and lovers, we have to be trustworthy ourselves. If we seek harmony, we have to refrain from creating unnecessary conflicts and drama. If we seek to manifest a successful business, we need to look at how we treat all the businesses with which we currently interact. Karma is a real thing. It is an extension of the Law of Attraction.

As you take stock of your life and begin filling your reserves with the cool, clean waters of positive thought and action, you may want to consider forgiveness. This is especially helpful if you've be wallowing in resentment, entertaining thoughts of revenge, or you've been holding grudges. Forgiveness is one of the most powerful tools you can use to detoxify your mind, heart, body and soul. In fact, a psychologist named Toussaint conducted a recent study correlating the ability to forgive with greater longevity and life span. How can forgiveness extend your life? Less stress! Forgiveness does not mean that you excuse another's inappropriate behavior, condone it, or that you will necessarily forget it. What it means is that you release the burden of those painful emotions, choosing to focus instead on the future. You are making the conscious decision to send all that toxic sludge from the past to the dumpster once and for all. It doesn't matter who was wrong or who was right. What counts is the quality of your internal peace, balance and happiness. You may want to send a note to your ex letting them know you wish them the best and bear them no ill will, or you might find it beneficial to write a letter to a family member that you haven't seen eye to eye with expressing your regrets and kind thoughts. This takes tremendous courage, but the rewards will be infinite. All that energy that was tied up with resentment can now be used to build your beautiful new life. Most of all, forgive yourself. This may be the hardest task to achieve, because often the person we are most angry at is ourselves. But again, letting go of those heavy, limiting emotions will transform and beautify your inner garden by leaps and bounds. Do your best to set things right, apologize to those you've harmed, and then make a firm decision to close the books on your past.

One of the side effects of this hard work is that you will find yourself being more compassionate and less judgmental of others. As your thoughts become more positive about your own life, you will be able to sow seeds of self-esteem in your family, your friends, co-workers and even in strangers. You become that golden fountain of love, and you no longer need to beg, borrow or steal from other people's gardens. You have everything you need within you. This is how we cultivate internal wealth. We are no longer emotional paupers, dependent on the whims or moods of others to make us feel good. Instead, we consistently generate our own good vibes like a self-sustaining star in the heavens. Our lives become miracles of generosity. We find that we can spare compliments and reassurance with everyone we come into contact with. Our fountain is overflowing. We have enough. We become known for our wisdom and our warmth. This in turn leads to all kinds of successes, from financial to personal. It's an inside job!

In the following chapters we will continue exploring in more depth the specific inner regions of your garden including mind, body and soul. As you gradually begin to manifest a mental, physical and emotional environment in tune with your deepest desires and aspirations, remember that constant upkeep is the key to your garden's long term health and beauty. Upkeep includes daily meditation, continued work with a counselor, life coach or therapist, the cultivation of hobbies and personal interests, exercise and all forms of self-investment, whether it means going on personal wellness retreats, going back to school, or embarking on a journey to explore your spirituality. It is not enough to just detox and then expect to coast along indefinitely. We have to commit to a complete lifestyle change, one in which we are constantly seeking to grow and to evolve. The golden fountain never stagnates. It is perpetually renewing itself with a clean, rushing supply of new energy that will always sustain us – if we put in the work.

Chapter 4: The Garden of the Mind

"You bring about what you think about.
You receive what you perceive."
– Cheyenne Bryant

Among the world's most beautiful sanctuaries, the Japanese garden stands out for its tranquility and exquisite design. Many Japanese gardens have at their center an immaculate shrine or a temple from which visitors can view the beauty of the outdoor ponds, as well as the bridges, sand, stones and lanterns. While the natural world outside the shrine is vulnerable to wind, rain and sunshine, the shrine remains a bastion of intense calm.

Our minds, like these sacred structures, are central to the beauty and efficiency of our lives. If the mind had a location, it would be in our brains, and although they weigh only three pounds, our brains are responsible for all our vital body functions, our dreams and all our thoughts. In the same way that we must condition our limbs and joints in order to avoid problems such as muscle atrophy, arthritis and osteoporosis, we have to exercise our brains, nurturing that grey matter with new information and skills and constantly challenging our minds to excel, improve and discard that which does not serve us. If we are in a rut in our lives, chances are this rut began as a mental one. But as you will learn, the brain possesses the remarkable ability to adapt and change, regardless of the time spent in a mental rut. If there is one thing you take away from this book, let it be the knowledge that the jumble of neurons and synapses in our brains responsible for all our life patterns is 100% malleable. Those brain wires are living tissue that can bend, bounce back, rejuvenate and regenerate. There is no amount of past damage, brokenness or pain that can prevent you from creating a new reality for your life. This is not just wishful thinking. Brain plasticity is a scientific fact!

Prior to the 1960's, scientists believed that the brain's pathways formed in infancy and childhood, and once that period was over, there was not much you could do to change things. They thought of the brain's wiring as a network set in stone, much like the shape of the human skull, or a person's height, neither of which can be altered. As technology improved throughout the years, brain scans revealed the startling evidence that our brains do not stop growing. In fact, they continue to grow and evolve right up until old age, unlike our limbs and skeletons.

This new information has led to breakthroughs for individuals who have suffered strokes and brain injuries, providing much needed hope for recovery. But it has also revolutionized the field of psychotherapy. Because of the plastic-like quality of our neural pathways, we don't have to wait years or months for change. Actions we take this very day create new pathways and new experiences, forming a new groove that we can return to immediately. This means that even if you have engaged in a bad habit or negative thinking for literally decades, in a single day you can begin reversing the process and start to feel the results immediately. This is very good news for those of us who fear we are too old, too weak or too broken to make drastic life changes. Research on brain plasticity shows us that it's much, much easier than we ever imagined. If we can picture qualities such as courage, patience, perseverance and gratitude as mental muscles, we can begin to see how every time we practice those traits, we strengthen that pathway. Before long, our brain simply bypasses the old messages of self-pity and fear, and follows a new road on its own. The key is just being willing to think about things in a new way, from a new perspective.

To illustrate this process with an example, let's consider an individual suffering from perfectionism. Every time this person achieves something, whether it be completing an online course, an exercise class or closing a deal at work, they immediate think, "I should have done better." They might look at their bodies in the mirror, and ignoring everything beautiful and functional, they focus exclusively on the one flaw they can observe. This type of thinking has been in effect for years, so it is almost unconscious, yet it breeds constant depression and feelings of inadequacy. It is a form of neurosis. The first step in healing is to become an observer of our minds, rather than allowing our minds to victimize us. We can step back and just notice the statement, "I should have done better/I should look better," and really hear it, maybe for the first time. We notice exactly when it pops up, and what happened right before the thought arose. Now the next time we hear it, we can make a conscious choice to repeat something different to ourselves. We can literally say out loud, "I did a great job" after completing a task or say, "I am beautiful" when we glance in the mirror. The reason it's good to say things out loud is that they are actions, rather than thoughts or feelings. Actions are always the most powerful agents of change. So write your affirmation on a post-it, program it into your phone, or record it and listen to it. As soon as we make this choice even a single time, the old pattern or pathway in the brain begins to literally die. It's like you are forging a new road in the forest. Even a single set of footsteps down that path will flatten the grass. Each time you reinforce your new phrase, "I did a great job/I am beautiful" that grass gets flatter. Before long, it's the only path you know! Your brain just automatically, effortlessly calls forth a positive statement rather than a negative one. It's been "rewired."

Another phrase to express the idea of a rut is "comfort zone." No breakthroughs will occur until you are willing to venture outside this mental sweet spot. If you are not uncomfortable, you're not growing! However, sometimes our comfort zone is being too hard on ourselves! I see many of my clients get trapped in the "should" zone. We "should be" richer, thinner, taller, smarter or more successful. We "should be" more feminine or more masculine, or we should come from a different background. The problem is that these expectations and demands are not coming from our authentic desire to be these things, but rather from an externally-motivated need to meet societal or familial obligations. It's natural to want to please our friends, co-workers, family members or children. But we can't allow anyone to put us inside a box or dictate our destinies. Be as BIG as you are! Do NOT compress or contort yourself because you do not fit in someone else's box. Create your own box! Shoulds can paralyze the mind, making it virtually impossible to explore any real self-discovery process. Until you accept yourself unconditionally just the way you are, true peace, happiness and harmony with others will remain unattainable. Remember that everything you feel, like or don't like is valid. Take everything you're told and everything you read with a grain of salt – even the advice in this book! "To Thine Own Self Be True!" Seek out your passion and abandon a life of boredom, dread and routine. An open mind is a free mind.

Three other weeds to uproot from the depths of your mind are worry, guilt and shame. Worry is one of the most corrosive and debilitating thought patterns known to mankind. It eats away like an acid at every good thing we try to cultivate, and often we feel totally powerless over it with no idea how to make it subside. Worrying is pointless and accomplishes absolutely nothing. There is nothing bigger than you, because you are creating your reality. Understand that worrying is a misguided attempt at self-preservation. Your mind worries as a way to warn you of impending doom. Worry is just fear dressed up in a thousand guises. Like many other traits we have discussed, worrying is a habit that we have repeated to the point where we think it's inevitable. But like all habits, we can change it.

First, we can ask ourselves if there is some piece of information that would help us gain clarity on a situation we are worried about. Sometimes all that is required is a trip to the library or Google, or a phone call to the IRS or the DMV. Clarity can dispel our worries and liberate our thoughts. We can ask people with more experience for help and guidance, or we can seek the counsel of a professional in the field. Information is power. Furthermore, worry comes from indecision. The cure to fear and worry is a firm decision! We do not worry over conditions once we have reached a decision to follow a definite line of action.

A lack of trust also produces worry. In these situations, we can look at our own track record and track records of others, and decide if this worry is based on fact. For all their unpredictability, people tend to repeat their behaviors. If you have always done pretty well on tests throughout the semester, it's reasonable to assume you will do pretty well on the final exam. You can trust yourself. As you continue working with a counselor, life coach or therapist, you will also gain more trust in others, and the compulsive worrying will gradually lessen.

Lastly, worry stems from a need to control the outcomes and results of situations. Once we release this chokehold on life, and surrender to the notion that we truly cannot control anything, it's much easier to live without worrying. We know that we are only responsible for our preparation, not the results. We can do everything in our power to assure a successful outcome, but at a certain point we have to let go and just have faith. Faith

is the opposite of fear and worry, and it requires a mental leap
– a leap right out of your comfort zone!

Equally draining to the mental environment are guilt
and shame. Guilt is the perception that we have done something bad or wrong, while shame is the feeling that we *are*
bad or wrong. While guilt and shame may sometimes help us
to remain accountable for our actions and drive us to make
amends, most of the time we are merely walking around punishing ourselves for all kinds of exaggerated wrongdoings, wallowing in a perverse form of emotional masochism. When we
constantly think guilty, shame-based thoughts, we attract more
shaming and punishment from the outside world due to the
Law of Attraction. Releasing this guilt and shame by letting
ourselves off the hook can be a huge step toward regaining personal power. Sometimes other people wrongfully accuse us, and
we take this guilt on as our own without examining whether it's
accurate. It is our right to disagree with their assessment of us.
Don't let anyone else dictate the quality of your inner life!

Misplaced shame and guilt often results when a child
experiences abuse at the hands of their caregivers. It is far
too overwhelming to consider that the people we trusted the
most in the whole world hurt us, and worse, that they hurt us
repeatedly, sometimes for years. Since we cannot process the
enormity of their transgressions, we often place blame on ourselves, which gives a sense of control and offers an explanation
for their misdeeds. If we were bad, rotten to the core, then the
abusers' actions made sense and we can accept what happened.

Learning to place the blame squarely on the shoulders of the responsible parties is a process that can take some time. It involves tremendous courage, as emotions begin to flood us, from grief to rage. But gradually we can come to hold our heads up high, knowing that the truth has set us free. The key is to understand that like worry, shame and guilt have no resolutions. They accomplish nothing. Once we acknowledge that shame is an outdated coping mechanism, we can stop taking it seriously. We stop giving it attention, and it withers and dies.

Now that we have cleared away many negative mental habits, how can we nourish our brains with new experiences? What kinds of activities are most challenging and invigorating to the brain? Let's start with reading books! Reading is a unique form of entertainment in that it assists your brain to develop the muscles of imagination. Unlike in a film or television show, where all the work is done for you, a book is a vehicle that allows each person their own experience, based on the mental images they create via the words on the page. As your mind pictures boats, buildings, civilizations, galaxies and all their inhabitants, as well as complex ideas and philosophies, you gain the power of innovation and creativity, skills you need to build a successful life. Now more than ever, reading books is an endangered activity, replaced by an addiction to all kinds of gadgets that promote instant gratification. Reading a novel, on the other hand, takes commitment and patience. It's a slow high that lasts for a lifetime rather than a few hours. There have been many recent studies that highlight the benefits of reading.

Researchers at the University of Sussex in the UK found that reading was more effective in relieving stress than herbal tea, exercise or listening to music. It also was effective in healing sleeplessness. In addition, the journal Neurology published a report that showed people who read books throughout their life had on average around a 65% higher retention of their memories and mental sharpness as they got older. Those that remained mentally sluggish found their minds deteriorating around 50% faster than their reading counterparts. Lastly, a Dutch journal conducted a study showing that reading boosted human empathy and the ability to relate to others and understand their problems.

Learning a new language, taking up or resuming an instrument, traveling and even exploring new recipes and exotic foods are all ways to keep your mind healthy, open and engaged. Even playing challenging games like chess or scrabble can bolster a sharp, agile mind. Going back to school can be daunting, both financially and emotionally, but no matter how old you are or how many reasons you can find to resist, education is a doorway to change. Not only are you exposed to points of view, cultures and lifestyles you wouldn't ordinarily encounter, but you develop follow-through, learning to finish what you start. Dealing with deadlines in an educational setting can be a good training ground for real-world pressure. Schools are also places where you can learn to take risks, while being buffered by your classmates and professors. These are just the side effects of pursuing education. The main effect is that you will increase your earning power, broaden your career choices and develop a track record of success. No matter what level you are at in your current work life, there is always more to learn!

Chapter 5: The Garden of the Body

"The body is the outermost layer of the mind."
– David Mitchell

As human beings, we are pure energy with varying degrees of density to our vibrations. Our physical bodies represent the slowest expression of our energy, in the most solid form. While the state of our physical health and appearance does depend primarily on the quality of our thoughts and beliefs, there is a reflexive quality to the mind-body relationship as well. Our bodies act as containers for our minds. Like the soil in a garden that surrounds the seeds of magnificent blooms-to-be, our bodies, along with our five senses, need to be nurtured and replenished regularly with rich, optimal nutrients, plenty of water, sleep and exercise, as well as loving touch – if we hope to function at our best.

We can call this dual self-care technique the "inside-out/outside-in" method, named after the two schools of theater training for actors. Our society tends to draw a sharp line between the two approaches, dividing healthcare into Western or Eastern medicine, and rarely do conventional physicians consult with psychologists to explore a holistic solution to total mind-body health. Here I offer you the best of both worlds, as I believe both paths are necessary for balance and integrity.

With the inside-out method, we focus on getting to the bottom of long-held mental distortions that have resulted in illness, disability and fatigue. We find that once we address the core issues of unworthiness, fear or self-hatred, the physical symptoms seem to miraculously clear up on their own. It has been shown that thinking positive thoughts releases endorphins in our brains, and that when we instead think negative thoughts, we release stress hormones. These stress hormones can wreak chaos on our physical bodies, causing weight gain, acne, fatigue and lowered immune response. Thus you can see that changing one's thought patterns is vitally important to maintaining a healthy physical body.

Simultaneously, we can use the outside-in method to uplift our thoughts, moods and feelings by improving physical self-care on all levels. It's hard to think clearly if you are drowning your brain cells in too much alcohol or junk food, and you probably won't feel too motivated to take action if you never exercise.

Let's first discuss inside-out healing. As a culture, we are obsessed with physical beauty, our weight and our desirability. These acute preoccupations fuel a host of billion-dollar industries from dieting to plastic surgery. Sadly, very few people concern themselves with inner beauty. Building character, developing inner peace and addressing the wounds of childhood rarely appeal to someone whose main goal is to look good in a bikini. But perhaps this would change drastically if more people realized that the image we project is literally a mirror reflecting our souls! We can make changes to our appearance all we want, but it will all be for nothing if we are ugly on the inside. No amount of surgery or makeup will be able to hide the twisted nature of our inner turmoil. We might begin an exercise routine and lose weight initially, but if we don't do the emotional work to understand the roots of our overeating, that weight will eventually return, no matter what we do about it in the physical world. In this case, we have merely dealt with the symptoms and not the cause. Beauty is a *way* of being! A life-style. It must be obtained internally prior to manifesting exter-nally. Additionally, perception plays a huge role in appearance. When we suffer from low self-esteem or self-hatred, we view our faces and bodies in a negative light, completely overlook-ing our assets and zooming in exclusively on flaws. That is what I mean when I say that your perception creates your reality.

For many of us, the neglect or abuse of our physical bod-ies began in childhood when our legitimate needs for affection, love and support were thwarted or outright denied to us.

In the case of the overeater, he or she may have learned to stuff down the pain with food, and this connection has accom-panied the individual throughout their lifetime. Now in the present, the person is trying to lose weight without addressing the real underlying cause of the coping mechanism. Once he or she can begin to let in love and nurturing from people rather than from a box of cookies, weight loss will naturally follow. The same goes for sleep disorders. Many kids grew up in vio-lent households, listening to screaming, too anxious to fall asleep. Now as adults, they can take sleep medication, but there are deeper issues at play that need to be addressed. Developing a sense of emotional safety and trust is integral to their healing process. And no pharmacist will be able to assist with this. This particular brand of sleep disorder must be healed from the inside out.

Some of the most serious health problems are a direct result of stress, and emotions such as worry, fear, anger, guilt and sadness can trigger stress hormones in the worst possible way. The list of conditions that stress can exasperate is over a page long and includes asthma, heart disease, irritable bowel syndrome, Alzheimer's, kidney problems, cancer, arthritis, diabetes and high blood pressure. Under the right circumstances, the "fight or flight" response can be a life-saver. After all, it is what ensured our survival as a species for eons. When faced with a dangerous threat, the adrenal glands secrete adrenaline and cortisol. Adrenalin ups our heart rate and blood pressure, while cortisol raises our blood sugar to give us that extra energy we need to fight off predators or run away. Usually these levels return to normal after the threat has passed, but when we are under chronic stress stemming from our unexplored emotion baggage, our system remains in a constant state of anxiety, overexposing us to these stress hormones which then cause damage.

The more traumatic a person's past has been, the more vulnerable they are to stress. Even simple events like getting a parking ticket or having a work conflict create enormous stress responses, inviting physical illness. This person lacks the ability to see difficult events as challenges, rather than catastrophes. Their perception is skewed, and the trickle-down effect in their body can have grave consequences. Healthy coping mechanisms have to be learned from scratch. These can include deep breathing and meditation, yoga, working with a counselor and learning to set proper boundaries with time. Regardless of the physical manifestations of the emotional issues, the work must begin within.

From the standpoint of outside-in work, even a quick look at our physical environments, especially our desks, can give us a lot of information about our lives. Do we live in a state of chaos, clutter or uncleanliness? Or do we wake up each day to beauty and order? You are a product of your environment, so choose your surroundings wisely. The clutter may be representing the mess inside you, but by creating external harmony in your home and office, you are signaling that you're ready to clean up internally as well. The same goes for how you dress. If you want to be successful, take pride in your appearance and honor yourself with beautiful garments. This can really make a world of difference in how you feel about yourself and provide an excellent boost to all the inner work you've been doing on self-esteem. Never underestimate the power of a well-groomed presentation! Getting a great haircut or getting your nails done won't solve all your problems, but it sends a message to yourself that you are worthwhile and deserve the best.

Nourishing our five senses can do wonders for our sense of well-being. By feeding our eyes, our ears, our noses, taste buds and sense of touch, we also feed our souls. When was the last time you feasted your eyes on a sunset, or a magnificent waterfall? Nature is a treasure chest of sensory vitamins, refreshing us on all levels. Our bodies crave Vitamin D in the form of sunlight, and the ion-charged ocean air increases our absorption of oxygen while boosting serotonin to lower stress levels. Today more than ever, maintaining a connection to nature has to be a conscious decision, as most of us are more and more removed from it through our jobs and urban lifestyles. But researchers at the University of Michigan have shown that workers who had more contact with nature showed a 20% improvement in concentration, attention span and memory. If you don't always have access to nature, you can still enjoy simple pleasures such as fresh flowers, bubble baths, or stargazing.

Another way to feed our senses is through art. Great paintings and musical works transport us to another level of consciousness, altering our perspective and filling up our reserves with doses of joy that we can draw on anytime we feel depleted. Creating a rich inner life nourished by the beauty of the world's greatest innovations gives us a sense of internal abundance and wealth that then overflows into the rest of our lives. Without delight, surprise or wonder, our souls can wither, withdrawing into a life of mundane tasks and obligations. You don't have to have a higher education to appreciate a beautiful poem, a jazz tune or the stained glass windows in a cathedral, either. These experiences belong to us all, making up our cultural history as human beings. There are many sources of inspiration in the world of art, and they are always available to act as your muse as you go about building your future.

We can learn to sooth our nerves and comfort our hearts with healing fragrances, engaging our sense of smell as an ally. Our sense of smell is directly connected to the part of our brain that controls emotion. Lavender oil helps alleviate stress and tension, and it has also been known to help with headaches and feelings of depression. Jasmine can promote a sense of optimism and rejuvenation, while reducing feelings of anger.

Food can sometimes become an overused method of comfort, but our taste buds also function as a portal into emotional bliss and well-being. Yes, we should all be eating more fruits and vegetables, but there is also a time and place for sweet indulgences that give our lives that extra sparkle! A small, delicious square of dark chocolate has a myriad of antioxidants that can lower cholesterol, improve memory, reduce the risk of cardiovascular ailments and help maintain healthy blood pressure. Eating chocolate releases phenylethylamine in our bodies, causing us to feel like we are falling in love. Chocolate also contains a THC-like compound that increases dopamine production in our brains. THC is found in marijuana, but you would have to eat 25 pounds of chocolate to get as high as you would smoking pot, so it's a much more benign form of mood-enhancement. Exotic spices can also affect us mentally and emotionally in all kinds of delicious ways. Turmeric, a relative of ginger long used in Chinese and Indian healing traditions, can work as an anti-depressant, and also as an anti-aging agent. Some scientists suggest that people who eat spicier foods take more risks! However you choose to explore your taste buds, discovering new cuisines is an adventure we can all enjoy, one that increases delight and nourishes curiosity.

And what about touch? When was the last time you treated yourself to a massage or a visit to the hot tub? Therapeutic touch – which includes acupuncture, reiki, acupressure, chiropractic care, craniosacral massage, rolfing, qigong and many other forms of energy healing – is known to assist with all kinds of ailments, from chronic pain to anxiety disorders. Infants that are not touched can die, and even as adults, we still need that regular human touch to function at our best. It's wonderful to enjoy touch with a lover or partner too, but being sensual with another person is difficult if we have never learned to first be sensual on our own. Also, our partners are not always available on call when we need them, so developing ways to nurture ourselves outside of a relationship is vital to our long term happiness.

Exercise is a form of self-care that has just as many mental and emotional benefits as physical ones. Just like any animal, if we don't flex our muscles, run and jump enough, we go stir crazy and our energy gets pooled up in our minds, causing anxiety, depression, paranoia or even rage. I'm not suggesting that every person join a gym or become a marathon runner. Sometimes all that's needed is to go dancing a few times a week at the club, or join a volleyball game on the beach. Find something you enjoy doing physically, even if it's just hiking or going for a bike ride. It will get your endorphins jumping and get oxygen to your brain. Playing sports can be a great way to meet other people in a fun, informal setting, too. All that matters is that you find a way to take pleasure in movement, expressing your aliveness through your body, the vehicle for your soul.

As we continue the healing process in the next chapter by exploring our relationship to not just our minds and bodies, but to our souls as well, you will hopefully begin to sense the interconnectedness of all the components in your garden. There is no such thing as compartmentalizing your life. Neglect your physical health and it will affect your mind, and mental neglect will cause your body to suffer. Repress the past, and it will reappear in the present, but linger too heavily in the past and the present will pass you by. A broken heart will cause problems with earning money, and failure to thrive in careers we are passionate about can cause our relationships to suffer. Only a holistic approach to wellness that addresses all these areas can succeed. So right now I invite you to pause for a moment to congratulate yourself on your progress so far. By reading each chapter deeply and taking these words to heart, you are preparing yourself for a life beyond your wildest dreams, one in which you experience a level of inner and outer congruence that you may have never thought was possible. A life in which you are completely free from all forms of mental and emotional slavery to self-defeating patterns and outdated strategies for survival. In no time, you will move beyond mere survival to shining at your full capacity as you were always meant to. Remember that champions are not crowned in a theatre or arena. They are crowned by the hard work, dedication, and resilience of the individual.

Chapter 6: The Garden of the Soul

*"We must go beyond the constant clamor of ego,
beyond the tools of logic and reason, to the still, calm
place within us:
the realm of the soul."*
– Deepak Chopra

The mind, body and soul work together in the human being just like the soil, water and sunlight in your garden. Harmony and interchange between each of these elements is integral to a happy and balanced life. To neglect the needs of our spirits is just as detrimental to our happiness as starving our bodies of food. We need to be nourished spiritually, for unlike animals or plants, our highly developed consciousness forces us to face the timeless conundrums of mortality, destiny, suffering and the meaning of existence. We have a need to understand our connection to others and our purpose in life. We also need a value system to guide us in our decision making process. To really grow and evolve, each of us must answer these philosophical questions for ourselves rather than internalize another's experience or beliefs, for rote memorization of religious doctrines can only go so far. At a certain point, only a personal experience of God will satisfy our spiritual appetites. We can think of our quest for spirituality as a grand adventure

– a journey towards defining our deepest, most authentic truth. This journey need not resemble anyone else's, either. It is a private pilgrimage all our own. It is what we make of it.

One of the best ways to meet God is to meditate. Meditation provides clarity and guidance. It helps us to be still enough so that God can obtain our undivided attention. Although God is always at work within us and for us, it is difficult for God to reach us on the deepest levels needed for us to fully receive our lessons and blessings when we are distracted by external forces. Furthermore, meditation is an exercise in self-control. Self-control is strength. If you cannot control your own mind, you cannot control anything! Meditation develops peacefulness and equanimity, and the more tranquil a man becomes, the greater is his success. Calmness is power.

Researchers at prominent hospitals and universities have discovered that meditation is linked with improved physical and mental health. Neuroscientists have demonstrated that meditation increases the brain's neuroplasticity, improving its ability to adapt, be flexible, change and cope. For this reason, meditation can ward off stress and all its effects like no other medicine. With stress-induced illness accounting for an average 80% of visits to healthcare providers in America, we cannot afford to overlook meditation as a potent, affordable and universally-accessible panacea. Dr. Herbert Benson of Harvard University remarked that, "Any condition caused or worsened by stress can be alleviated through meditation." It can even help with depression, chronic pain, high blood pressure and immune response. A 2005 study correlated an increase in cortical thickness with the practice of meditation, indicating that meditators were aging slower, had stronger memories and were capable of higher levels of concentration.

Exactly how you meditate is up to you, but there are some guideposts that can be helpful. Focusing on the repetition of the breath is at the heart of most meditation practices. This brings you into the present, centers and calms your mind, and locks you into the soothing rhythms of both your inner and outer environments. You can focus on your breath, your heartbeat or your pulse, or the nurturing sounds of nature, such as ocean waves, birds, the rustle of the wind in the trees or the sounds of a bonfire. You can meditate while gazing into a beautiful sunset or you can meditate through chanting sacred mantras such as "Om," which some say represents the sound of the Universe. Meditation works best from a comfortable position, such as sitting on a pillow or even lying down in the grass. It is always good to practice in a quiet, secluded place where cell phones and other media are turned off and the lighting is non-invasive. Pleasant aromas such as incense or scented candles can offer additional relaxation to the senses. If you need extra assistance, there are all kinds of videos, CD's and even phone apps that can aid you to meditate and make it more fun. Meditating in a group is especially beneficial, as you draw and absorb all the positive energy around you, soaking it up like a sponge. However, meditating alone is effective as well. Like exercise, meditation is a skill that must be built up over time. It's best to start small, with as little as five minutes daily, and then build on that until meditation becomes a more habitual response to everyday obstacles and stressors. It can be performed any-where, even in your cubicle at work. After all, as long as we are alive and breathing, we might as well breathe mindfully.

As meditation is widely practiced in Eastern philoso-phies and religions, it is worth exploring the Buddhist notions of Metta, Karuna, Mudita and Upekkha. These are the primary goals of Buddhist meditation, and even if you are not attracted to Buddhism per se, they can be helpful concepts to incorpo-rate into your spiritual practice. Metta means "loving kindness" or "friendliness," and can be compared to the similar Christian concept of "goodwill" or blessing oneself and others. It is the simple practice of wishing all beings well, and being kind to everyone that crosses your path. As we know from the Law of Attraction, you will reap what you sow. Treating others as you wish to be treated is the Golden Rule, after all. Wishing others well makes us feel happier and healthier, and it increases our self-esteem. We also automatically expect the same from other people when we do this, and that makes us more open to part-nerships, relationships and success in business. Sometimes it's hard to feel loving kindness towards certain people, whether they be politicians we abhor, family members we disagree with, or institutions that have snubbed us. But by blessing all these, we can begin to overcome our inclination to judge others and condemn them. We start to give people the benefit of the doubt and understand that everyone is just trying to be happy in their own way. This translates into greater self-love and self-accep-tance, because we are all one.

The concept of Karuna relates to compassion. This is an emotion that spans across all religions and spiritual practices. Compassion means to "feel with others," to feel their pain as your own. In our capitalist society, we tend to view competition as the norm, along the lines of "survival of the fittest." But Dacher Keltner from the Greater Good Science Center maintains that we have survived as species due to compassion for one another, not antagonism. He makes the point that the phrase "survival of the fittest" was borrowed from its evolutionary context and reinterpreted by the Social Darwinists to condone racial and economic injustice. Revealing another perspective, NYU researcher Jonathan Haidt demonstrated that businesses and corporations not only ran better, but they made a lot more money when compassion was at the core of their dealings with both employees and clients. It's also something we can learn to feel for ourselves when we are struggling or suffering. Compassion for self is different from self-pity. With self-pity, we lose perspective, thinking we are the only person with problems and we have it the worst. It isolates us and drains us of energy. Compassion, on the other hand, lifts us up, empowering our spirits and reminding us that we are connected to every other living thing.

Mudita is a word that translates to "feeling joy in the joy of others." It's the opposite of schadenfreude, which means taking pleasure in the suffering of others. Mudita can really help us with jealousy and the tendency to compare ourselves and come up short. When we rejoice in others' joy, we affirm that happiness and success are abundant. If someone else experiences some happiness, it doesn't mean they are robbing us of our share. That kind of scarcity thinking really diminishes us and detracts from our efforts to stay positive and proactive.

Finally, upekkha refers to equanimity. The ability to ride out both good and bad days without allowing oneself to become discouraged or over-elated is one of the greatest benefits of meditation. Instead of experiencing ourselves as a tiny rowboat that is tossed and flung by overpowering waves, we become the big, calm, confident ocean liner that remains steady on its course despite the winds. Everything is polarity. You cannot experience victory and not experience defeat. Life is about experiences, and you WILL experience both spectrums of life. Embrace this with the perception of joy.

Where meditation is God speaking to us, prayer is when we speak to God. I often say that every word and thought is a prayer, but we also need to set aside time to pray in more formal ways. This is a chance for us to express our gratitude for all the good in our lives, to ask God's protection for our friends and family, and to set our intention for peace, both in our lives and throughout the Earth. It's also a time when we can express remorse for actions or words we may regret. In short, prayer is an essential ingredient to healing, and it has been practiced as such for the last 5000 years in cultures all over world, whether they be Buddhist, Christian, Jewish, Hindu, Muslim or Other. There are as many ways to pray as there are people. For some Native American societies, dancing was a type of prayer! Prayers can also be expressed as songs, pictures or through unique actions like fasting. The bottom line is that prayer is a creative act, and need not be limited by traditional avenues. Even if you have trouble believing that prayer accomplishes anything external, there are close to 300 studies conducted by researchers and scientists that demonstrate the effects of prayer on our health, well-being and mood. In his book, *The Healing Power of a Healthy Mind*, psychologist Dr. William Backus demonstrated how prayer bolstered the immune systems of patients suffering from AIDS, and Dr. Martha Highfield, an RN, published an article in the journal *Cancer Nursing* showing that individuals with chronic pain significantly improved when they engaged in prayer. The *Journal of Behavioral Medicine* also reported that high blood pressure was alleviated when people engaged in group prayer. Prayer, like everything else, is a form of energy, so it can be directed in powerful ways that will complement and enhance all the other forms of self-care that you practice.

The result of continued meditation and prayer is that we develop intuition, a powerful sense of inner guidance that begins to function on its own. We start to trust our gut feelings about people, work situations and even what foods are right for our bodies. We stop doubting and start listening. Our intuition becomes a kind of GPS system that we can use to navigate even the most challenging situations in life. And every time we do listen, we grow our integrity and our confidence, because we no longer have to check in with all kinds of external authorities. We go straight to God within us. We develop the strength to stand alone with our convictions, even if everyone else disagrees with us. There are hundreds of other benefits of prayer and meditation, of course. You will just have to experiment and find out on your own which ones are your favorites!

Another important aspect of a rich soul life is the concept of doing service. This can be anything, from volunteering for worthy causes, to mentoring youth, to lending a helping hand to a neighbor. Volunteering is a great way to improve job skills, train for a new career or network, all while contributing to the greater good. When you become a mentor, you share your experience and knowledge with a younger generation, investing in young minds and hearts, which are among our greatest resources as a species. There have been some highly successful mentoring programs that have helped thousands of people to succeed and prosper. One excellent program is called SCORE, which matches retired businessmen and businesswomen with would-be entrepreneurs. The retirees are celebrated for their expertise and wisdom, and this can be very important in a culture that tends to dispose of older workers and devalue them. The Big Brothers Big Sisters of America mentoring program has also changed many lives for the better. The kids that spent quality time with their mentor were almost 50% less likely to get involved in using drugs or dropping out of school, and given the dire statistics of our public education system, (about one in four students will drop out of high school,) these figures show tremendous hope and value. Volunteering our time gives us a sensation of abundance. We may initially feel like we have nothing to spare, but through acts of service, we learn that we have much more to offer than we ever imagined. This builds our self-esteem, strengthens our connection to our communities and fills our minds and hearts with positive energy. Again, by practicing generosity, we are attracting a similar energy back from the universe.

The social, vocational and emotional benefits of giving back are not the only rewarding byproducts. There can also be significant health benefits to generosity. Researchers at the University of Michigan demonstrated that when compared to non-volunteers, those that donated their time on a regular basis tended to live longer. Their generosity and altruism actually added years to their lives! In her wonderful book *29 Gifts: How a Month of Giving Can Change Your Life,* author Cami Walker was suffering from Multiple Sclerosis, a degenerative disease that affects the brain and the spine. Cami was at the end of her rope, immobilized and plagued by depression when a healer from Africa gave her some unusual advice. The woman told her to "give to others for 29 days." The gift could take any form and be directed towards any person, even strangers. It didn't have to be expensive or elaborate. It could be as simple as calling a sick friend, watering someone's plants or walking an elderly person to the library. The book relates that in less than one month, Cami's life changed radically. Her health, mood and entire outlook was completely rearranged. She regained her ability to walk and was even able to take on a part-time job, something that had seemed virtually impossible just a few weeks earlier!

As you continue to cultivate the garden of your soul with the beautiful flowers of integrity, honesty, patience and humor, you will find that your new plants give off their own seeds, and you can begin sharing your supply. Now that your garden is clean, fruitful and peaceful, there is a fertile internal space to attract healthy relationships of all kinds. In the next few chapters, we will begin to explore the challenges and rewards of opening up your garden gates to visitors!

Chapter 7: The Garden Gates

"Shared joy is a double joy; shared sorrow is
half a sorrow."
– Swedish Proverb

Healthy human relationships are not only a source of joy and support, they are also chemically necessary for our survival. When we experience trust, community and affection, our brain releases the hormone oxytocin, which wards off stress, depression, fear and anxiety. We may need to take time for solitude in order to heal, but ultimately we are not meant to live in isolation. God made us social creatures. However, if we have experienced abuse, neglect or trauma, or have ever been betrayed by our fellow human beings, healthy relationships may seem like rocket science. What's important to remember is that as the gatekeeper of your garden, you are now in a position to decide who gets in and out. You have worked hard to tend the soil, plant the flowers and purify the fountain, and now you get to choose your visitors. You are no longer a victim, at the mercy of your caregivers. You are an adult, and you have choices. Just knowing this is empowering, because it helps to lift the fear of intimacy, which is really just the fear that people will hurt us.

Boundaries are what create order and beauty in our gardens. Each of our crops has its own plot, protected from the wind and storms. Our pond has a gate around it so that our ducks don't get lost. And our front gates prohibit strangers and freeloaders from trampling on our flowerbeds. Learning to establish healthy boundaries in relationships can feel like a tall order if we grew up being violated. We might feel like any attempt to separate or differ from another is an invitation for conflict, and conflict, we fear, leads to abandonment. Conversely, we may fear enmeshment, suffocation or being controlled by others and thus keep our distance, putting up walls. In either case, whether our boundaries are too weak or too strong, we are starving ourselves from the joy that other people can bring into our lives.

Fortunately, there are some great ways we can overcome these fears. The first is to cultivate patience and take our time getting to know people. This may sound obvious, but thanks to our oversaturation by movies and TV where all the characters only have a few hours to bond, we mistakenly try to accelerate our connections instead of giving them time to grow organically. Friendships, romantic partnerships and business liaisons all take time to form, just like juicy fruits on a tree. The ones that flare up brightly in an instant, also burn out just as fast. So if you have trust issues honor your hesitations and just take small baby steps towards socializing. Spending 20 minutes having coffee with a new friend is a great start. You want to surround yourself with people who inspire you, who have what you want; people that stretch you and challenge you to be your best; people who celebrate you, not merely tolerate you. So these are the clues to look for as you are inviting a new soul into your circle of wealth. You have the right to be discerning and practice good judgment. This is not the same as being judgmental. If you decide that someone is too angry for you to be around, you're not condemning them or saying that their anger is 'wrong.' You're just saying that it's wrong *for you* and the kind of peaceful mental environment you are trying to cultivate. There is a big difference.

Good boundaries take form physically, verbally and emotionally. Through meditation and counseling, we can learn what feels acceptable to us in each area. Then it becomes our job to let others know where our limits are. This requires courage and honesty, but most of all, communication. Otherwise we become imprisoned by resentment, misunderstanding and fear. Some of the reasons we don't speak up are due to codependence and people-pleasing. We keep our mouths shut when someone cracks an off-color joke, or we turn a blind eye when someone tells a white lie. We let a friend dominate the conversation, even though we have a lot to say. Over time, this silence erodes our self-esteem because we're not being authentic. Our relationships become merely empty shells, because we are not sharing our truth. Without honesty, there is no intimacy. Keeping silent about our needs, desires, feelings and opinions is also manipulative, because we are trying to achieve a desired result in an indirect way. We want the other person to like us, so we put on a mask. We pretend to be someone we're not.

In addition to trust, communication and honesty, stable long-lasting friendships are built by practicing active listening. This means not only really listening to the words people say, but listening to their body language, their silences and their actions. A lot of times we have information and ideas in our heads that cloud our perception of what the other person is trying to say. We might interpret someone raising their voice as a sign of anger, because that's what it always meant in our family. However a raised voice could also be a sign of enthusiasm or excitement and not necessarily something negative. If you are in doubt, you can always ask a question to verify that you're receiving the right message. It's also important to listen without already creating a counterargument in your head. If you are thinking about what you're going to say while someone else is talking, then you're not really listening! (If your cell phone is beeping, or you're typing on the computer at the same time, you are also not actively listening.) It's important to refrain from reacting to or judging what another person is saying. Create space between the event and the reaction! Successful people stop, think of the outcome and breathe before they react! And not everyone is looking for you to offer them a solution. To make someone feel heard, sometimes all that's required is a simple statement of reflection, like, "I hear that you are really hurting right now."

Other habits that lead to successful relationships include the ability to apologize, the ability to keep your word, and the ability to keep a secret. If there's one thing every adult should learn, it's how to simply say, "I'm sorry," when they make a mistake. It's so simple and can save so much time and heartache. But there are good and not so good ways to make amends. It's usually best to avoid apologizing if you don't mean it. If you say you're sorry and then repeat the same behavior, you diminish your reliability with that person and they may now have no reason to trust you when you attempt to make a sincere amends in the future. Another type of apology that doesn't work is where you remind the other person of what they did wrong. You try to explain and justify your behavior rather than just taking responsibility for your part. Apologizing doesn't mean the other person is off the hook or that they're now free from guilt. It just means that you value the friendship enough to swallow your pride and admit fault. It also means you value your mental environment and don't want to contaminate it with resentment, grudges, guilt or shame.

Keeping your promises, your word and your commitments is absolutely mandatory for building trust. If you don't plan to attend a friend's party, it's best to be honest rather than say you'll be there and flake. If you really can't show up for someone, it might be time to examine why you have that person in your life in the first place. Keeping your word increases your self-esteem and confidence. It also breeds a sense of security, because you know *you* are reliable.

Keeping a friend or loved one's secrets is another building block towards trust and intimacy. This doesn't only apply when someone directly tells you to keep information in confidence. It also means not relating to others events or discussions that would be embarrassing or painful for your friend. A juicy story might be fun to tell when you're bored at work, but entertainment at the expense of another's pain is no way to spice up your life. Sometimes you become privy to a secret that alarms you. A friend might divulge that they are cheating on their spouse, or that they've stolen something. Your first instinct might be to go blurt this information out to another party, but ideally you have enough respect for your friend that you allow them to come clean in their own way. You can tell them how you feel, and if you can't abide their revelations you can even end the friendship, but don't break their confidence. Everyone makes mistakes. If you do need to discuss the situation, speaking with a neutral party such as a therapist or life coach is the best option. (The only exception to this is if someone you know threatens to harm themselves or another. Then you are obligated to tell others immediately and get help.)

As you become a better gatekeeper to your garden, you may have to deal with the end of certain relationships. In order to live peacefully with integrity and joy, you may find that you can no longer abide a certain family member's negativity, or you may have to end a friendship that doesn't feel safe. There is a lot of grief associated with severing ties, but change and growth is a natural part of life. Trees shed their leaves, snakes shed their skins, and from time to time we need to do a spring cleaning in our relationship department, clearing out space to make room for new, more nourishing associations. This need not be dramatic or painful. You can detach with love, by sending a silent prayer or blessing to the person you are ending things with. There is always something you can be grateful for in every relationship, even if it's only the new awareness they have brought into your life that you deserve better! Honoring others even while separating from them reinforces our self-esteem and self-respect. We avoid name-calling, gossip or retaliation, because those things only intoxicate us, exposing us to these harms as well. Let the refining and improving of your own life keep you so busy that you have little time to criticize others. See the other person as your teacher, and thank them.

Now that you have mastered the art of gatekeeping by applying these new skills and insights to your platonic relationships, you are ready to explore a deeper level of closeness with a significant other. Romantic relationships flourish best when we have a foundation of community in loving friends, family members and colleagues. Day by day, our garden grows more lush, vibrant and abundant. Our lives expand, and we welcome this growth with open arms and a grateful heart!

Chapter 8: The Lovers' Garden

"Lovers don't finally meet somewhere.
They're in each other all along."
– Rumi

While platonic relationships may be compared to the lovely lilies, irises, tulips or snapdragons in our gardens, romantic relationships are a different type of flower; they are our treasured roses. Their fragrance is just a little more potent and intoxicating than the others – and sometimes they come with very sharp thorns! Roses bloom a little later in the summer, but no garden would be quite as beautiful without them.

Romantic relationships invite us to explore a deeper level of intimacy and vulnerability than any other kind of partnership. According to the Greek playwright Aristophanes, humans once had two bodies and three sexes, but upon angering the great god Zeus, they were split into two parts, condemned to forever search for their missing half and the feeling of wholeness. This is an ancient myth, of course, but it speaks to the deep longing we feel inside to be reunited with a soul mate or soul twin. We desire to lose ourselves in another, erasing the boundaries between consciousness to gain a momentary reprieve from our aloneness. What Aristophanes failed to mention, is that only two wholes can make a whole relationship!

While it's natural to search for fulfillment from another person, romance is only truly sustainable when both people are already complete.

The search for love has been the subject of countless films, books, poems, novels, plays and works of art, and these external cues combined with our personal beliefs and experiences about romance formed in childhood create our expectations for our own lives. Like everything else, love partnerships reflect our inner landscape and operate according to the Law of Attraction. Every relationship in our lives is a mirror of what is going on inside us! This plays out in many ways. Because our systems seek balance, if we have not done the internal work to clear away our wounds, we will draw certain types of people to us in order to heal. We don't heal in a vacuum, so if we're not familiar with therapy, mediation or visiting a life coach for instance, we are going to try to heal through the people we date. If we are broken inside, we will attract a broken partner in an unconscious attempt to address our own problems. If we ourselves need fixing, we will attract someone we think we can fix. We might scratch our heads wondering why we always choose such "losers," but instead of placing the blame outwards, we can just ask ourselves what lessons the relationship holds for us and which of our partner's qualities that we dislike seems familiar and why. As the old saying goes, "If you spot it, you got it." If we're settling for someone who belittles us, abuses us or cheats on us, we have to ask ourselves why we would allow someone to dishonor us in this way. The reason usually stems from trauma we sustained in our youth, and it has to be addressed head-on before we can start attracting a kind and loving soul. Remember that it's not your job to seek love, but to break down the barriers that keep you from giving and receiving love in a healthy way.

We often hear the phrase, "Opposites attract." Again, this relates to the idea that our partners are clues, revealing more about ourselves and where we need to focus our inner work. Opposites often appear in our lives to provide us with a quality we lack that is needed to reach our goals. For instance, we may need to be more assertive, so we draw to us a person who is dominant and ultra confident. We "borrow" this quality from them until we begin to develop it authentically within us. No doubt the partner also gets something from the exchange and is unconsciously seeking a certain quality that *they* lack, such as gentleness, or compassion. The union awakens both lovers to the unexplored areas of their personality, but once those lessons are learned, the relationship may quickly dissolve. This is natural, because while opposites do attract, they cannot sustain one another long term. They bloom only briefly, like seasonal flowers rather than perennials.

Only similarities can sustain a long term partnership. Having the same values, interests and lifestyle as your love makes for a harmonious relationship. You feel in synch with the other person and when both are healthy, you constantly exchange positive energy, invigorating and inspiring one another. You experience companionship and peace, rather than that drama that we so often mistake for "sparks." Sometimes these drama-free relationships seem a little boring compared to all the intrigue and rollercoasters of the past, but stability and harmony at home go a long way in supporting all your other goals in life. Eventually we realize that love should not bring us pain, strife or distress. Rather our partnership should reflect cooperation, mutual respect and real caring. When both people are working from a place of love, they're opening their chakras up to both receiving and giving. There is no winner or loser. Both people are enriched through love.

Speaking of winning and losing, competition within relationships is one of the worst forms of self-sabotage. This can be common, however, for to some degree, we are all pitted against one another in the workplace. Some women spend their lives fighting to gain legitimacy and respect in their chosen male-dominated field. When they come home, it can be difficult to let go of this struggle and remember that their male partner is an ally and not a foe. Similarly, some men feel emasculated or threatened by successful women and may react competitively rather than supportively, especially if they feel they are being talked down to. (We are speaking about heterosexual relationships, but there are plenty of parallels in gay partnerships as well.) Competition erodes trust and friendship and repels intimacy. These lovers are turning tools into weapons. Instead of praising their partner and affirming all the good they see, they allow insecurity to negate the chance to form a deeper bond. If competition is eating away at your love, start finding ways to heal the rift. Admit your competitive feelings to your partner and you may find yourselves relating and laughing about it. Compliment your partner. Find activities to do together that build you up as a team. If both are in a place of self-awareness and gratitude, two strong people can become a power couple, rather than opponents. Power couples use their competitiveness to fuel ingenuity and new ideas. They don't get hung up on keeping score, or who is in control. They brainstorm together about career moves, find opportunities to pool their talents and even exercise together. They constantly communicate. And lastly, when they encounter other power couples, they leave competitiveness aside and see what they can learn and how they can contribute. Life becomes a win-win miracle of ever-increasing opportunity, rather than a downward spiral of jealousy and conflict.

Another huge source of self-sabotage in relationships is waiting around for people to change. What you see at the present moment is as good as it may ever get. Stop falling in love with the "potential" person. Start falling in love with who the individual truly is! If you are unable to love them for exactly who they are right now at this moment, then it is best you begin creating a new circumstance. Remember that nothing your partner is doing is personal. We all have our patterns, and if you gained the ability to look back on your lover's past relationships, you would see that the behavior they exhibited with you is the same behavior they have always exhibited. It's also exactly how they are going to treat their new partner, because it is very rare that people change. If someone speaks very poorly and unkindly about their ex while you're getting to know them, this is a red flag! It won't be long before this man or woman is badmouthing you too.

Sometimes the reason a relationship doesn't quite work is because the two parties involved speak different love languages. This is an important concept to understand, because it explains the mystery as to why two wonderful individuals might not necessary make a cohesive unit, despite the fact that both are fairly healthy. A love language is the way that we communicate affection, support, desire and passion. Marriage counselor Gary Chapman coined the term and wrote several books on the topic. He explained that there are five types of love expressions: words of affirmation, acts of service, receiving gifts, quality time and physical touch. If one person's love language is verbal, while the other's is acts of service, there will be a significant gap in their understanding of each other. Try as they might, their best intentions don't seem to land. For instance, one partner may being saying, "I love you," but the other needs to experience this as an action, like helping to make dinner. Love may be present, but it doesn't *feel* like love. After a while, this can really be draining. Learning to compromise and speak another love language is possible, however. It just takes a lot of commitment and effort. There is a lot of overlap, of course. You may 'speak' touch, quality time and words as signs of affection, and if your partner shares one of these in common, then there is a place to build from. If there really is no common ground however, and your partner ONLY speaks the language of receiving gifts, then you will struggle and it might be best to find someone more compatible.

Unlike the person who gets into relationships to solve internal issues, there are some folks that avoid relationships entirely, believing they are better off alone. Sometimes when the pain is too great, it just feels easier to shut down internally and keep everyone out. Some may use fantasy, or retreat into relationship substitutes like porn or promiscuity, but essentially their chief goal is to avoid intimacy. Unfortunately when we shut out love, we also shut out everything else, including many blessings and opportunities. We protect ourselves from a broken heart, but we also deprive ourselves of joy, fun, connection and the chance to grow as a person. We inflict on ourselves a lonely state of isolation, punishing ourselves for our own vulnerability that led to being hurt. For this person, the fear of betrayal, rejection and the unknown is just too great to support any real risk-taking. In order to learn to trust again, working with a life coach or psychotherapist is the first step. A good relationship coach or guide can help navigate the uncertain terrain of dating, helping the shut-down individual to gently open up to love. Being part of a loving community, whether that is through church, a support group, a school or a club, also creates a solid foundation from which the seeds of romantic relationships can begin to sprout and flower. In short, a broken heart must be healed holistically, from the inside out.

With a better understanding of personal relationships now under your belt, your garden is fast becoming a luxurious retreat full of abundance and human warmth. You are learning to juggle self-care with the demands of caring for others. You are giving and receiving love, and your energy is overflowing. It is now time to take all these victories and new skills and venture into another area of your garden. Your life's work!

Chapter 9: The Vocational Garden

*"I've learned that making a 'living' is not the same
thing as 'making a life.'"*
– Maya Angelou

"Always do what you are afraid to do."
– Ralph Waldo Emerson

The vocational garden is a metaphor for the part of our lives that we devote to career, work, accomplishments and earning. We might say that the vocational garden is where we plant the vegetables. Becoming a wealthy, healthy professional, in every sense of the word, requires that we draw on all the other skills and coping mechanisms we have learned in this book, plus some new ones.

The Law of Attraction is as strong as ever in our work lives. We consistently draw to us the clients, bosses, coworkers and customers that resonate with our internal energy. We manifest our core beliefs about work and money as outer circumstances, so although it seems counterintuitive, adjusting our attitudes is the key to improving our personal economy. In other words, our pocketbooks are proportionate to our internal wealth.

Part of internal wealth is joy. If we hate the work we do, or merely tolerate it, no amount of money can make us feel rich. Discovering your passion in life and turning it into a source of income doesn't come easy for every person. Some of us were deprived of encouragement at home and then again at school. We may have had to make personal sacrifices for the good of our families, brushing aside our dreams for another day. Others of us have always known what we wanted to do, but let fear incapacitate us, justifying our cowardice with excuses about 'being practical' and paying the bills. How many of us have formulated a plan to get to point A by first visiting B, C and D? There is no reason to have a plan B, because it distracts from plan A. Stop pursuing a life that does not belong to you!

At the beginning of this book I talked about the power of formulating a vision. Ask yourself what your ideal job and work situation feels like. Where do you work? What do you do all day? Do you see yourself working with other people? Objects? Ideas? Do you work with words or raw materials? How much money do you want to earn? If you never ask yourself these questions, you will simply wind up following the path of least resistance and getting a job that's convenient, or passed on to you through your family. I invite you to dream BIGGER! Set a goal so high that it would blow your mind to achieve it! Do exactly what you want, how you want to, and when you want to! If you want something, GO GET IT! The only thing stopping you is the negative chatter in your own head. From today forward, you are going to devote yourself to embracing your passion. Forget drudgery. Work should be something you long to wake up to every day. Your occupation should nourish you physically, mentally and spiritually. Once you fully believe you can experience that kind of life, you are one step closer to making it happen. Remember that enthusiasm is the fertilizer that will insure the rapid growth of your dreams for the future.

Fear of success and fear of failure are two of the most common reasons we avoid pursuing our dreams. They are really two sides of the same coin. They both involve fear, after all! We know that when we harbor fear in our hearts, there is no room for love. And without love, success is hard to come by.

Let's first talk about fear of failure. Many of us are paralyzed by the thought of making a mistake. But there is practically nothing you can learn to do in life that you won't first fail at many times before succeeding. Once you understand that failure is a necessary step on the path to success, it stops being such a big deal. It just becomes part of the process. We always obtain more from a bad experience than no experience. When you learned to walk, you fell hundreds of times, just as Thomas Edison made 1000 light bulbs before he designed one that actually worked. Babe Ruth was famous for breaking the record for most home runs and the highest batting average, but the same year, he also broke the record for most strike outs. The explanation is simple: in order to hit a home run, you have to be willing to strike out – a lot! Any sales job will teach you that the number of "yes's" you receive is contingent on the number of "no's". More rejections mean more sales, because you need to eliminate a certain number of people to find the ones that want your goods or services. Since almost every job involves some aspect of sales, it's good to start challenging yourself to seek out rejections. You may want a raise, but you might have to ask for it 3 times before you get it. If you can't bear to hear "no" even one time, it will be unlikely that you get that raise. As Bruce Jenner put it, "The ability to grow is directly related to the amount of insecurity you can take in your life."

There are hundreds of wildly successful people who started off failing. The author Stephen King, now a celebrity and very rich man, had his first book rejected 30 times. James Joyce and even Dr. Seuss were also rejected by publishers over 20 times. Steven Spielberg was rejected from film school twice! The renowned actor Sidney Poitier was told he should be a dishwasher after his first audition, and the late great Robin Williams was named "least likely to succeed" by his high school. No matter what your goals are, it's good to start compiling a list of success stories that reinforce the concept of overcoming obstacles. You might be afraid you are too old, too young, too poor, too ugly or too untalented to do XYZ, but chances are there are dozens of role models you can find right now who did exactly what you want to do with even greater odds against them than you are currently facing. What soon becomes apparent is that there are literally no limits to what you can achieve or accomplish. The only limits are the ones we place on ourselves out of fear. Eventually these fears turn out to be excuses to stay in a state of perpetual longing, boredom, poverty and inertia. No one will give you opportunities on a silver platter. There are just too many people in the world for that. You have to create opportunities for yourself! To become successful you must be a person of action, for the strength of your effort is the measure of the result. You cannot get anywhere without persistence. There is a great saying that goes, "I'd rather have a life of 'ooh wells' than a life of 'what ifs.'" Even if you shoot for the moon and you miss, you will reach the stars.

Another of our greatest fears is that we have nothing of value to contribute. We look at the field we want to enter and see it is already filled with talented people. We compare ourselves and fall short. Self-doubt cripples us and destroys the pleasure we might have taken in pursuing our favorite profession. What we forget is that each of us is utterly unique in all the world. No one will ever occupy the same space as us or have quite the same perspective. The very best tool we have as workers is our originality. God made each us just like snowflakes. All we have to do is show up and be our authentic selves. This contribution is worth its weight in gold, because by expressing our one-of-a-kind essence, we help expand and enrich the human experience. There is a beautiful quote by the modern dancer Martha Graham that goes, "There is a vitality, a life force, an energy, a quickening that is translated through you into action, and because there is only one of you in all time, this expression is unique. And if you block it, it will never exist through any other medium and will be lost." There can never be too many voices in the choir. Each voice only adds more beauty to the chorus. If you are afraid that there is not enough room for another actress, another lawyer, another writer, another comedian or another therapist, gently remind yourself that God doesn't give us aspirations only to slam doors in our faces. There is a reason you feel a certain calling. In the words of Iyanla Vanzant, "The biggest privilege in your life is to be yourself."

Fear of success can sometimes be more difficult to heal, as it has its origins in shame. Many gifted children were ridiculed or punished for exhibiting extraordinary abilities. We may have been conditioned not to outshine our insecure parents or siblings, or we may have been treated as a nuisance by a teacher for raising our hand too many times in class. We might even fear that harm will come to us, as in the case of a woman losing weight who fears the attention she might receive being in a more attractive body. We may be afraid that if we shine, we will wind up alone, abandoned and unloved. Fitting in becomes more important than being true to our God-given talents. When we shrink and contort ourselves to please other people, to avoid their wrath or to placate their jealousy, the self-betrayal wounds us to our core. We get sick and depressed. Hiding out is simply not sustainable in the long term. You won't start living until you stop caring about what folks think of you! Playing dumb and staying small is really just the mirror image of exalting ourselves above others. Neither extreme is particularly conducive to a happy, purposeful life. The only way out is to embrace a spiritual approach to success in general. We can see our gifts as coming from God, and practice gratitude and generosity. We can focus on helping others, rather than on the ego.

The Vocational Garden

One of biggest ways we can sabotage ourselves at work is by mismanaging our time. Procrastination, sloth and 'time drunkenness' can all contribute to missed opportunities and stagnant earning. We are often at odds with time, feeling like we never have enough of it, and that it's running out. To a certain extent, this is true. Time is finite and cannot be replenished. We have a limited amount of time on this earth to fulfill our life purpose, but instead of using this as a reason for self-pity or apathy, we can learn to honor time as a precious resource and use it wisely. We have to learn to organize our time around our deepest most authentic priorities, and shed the activities that don't serve our highest good. In the same way we prune our garden, selecting just the right seeds to plant, we can prune our schedules, snipping away certain activities in favor of others that are more important to us. Instead of being victims of time, we can become co-creators with time, embracing it as a partner that provides helpful boundaries. Time constraints are not always a bad thing. Sometimes they help us to focus better and get to the point faster.

Procrastination has many causes. For some it stems from crippling perfectionism. Sometimes it is others that set these impossibly high standards for us, other times it's we ourselves who create unrealistic expectations and punish ourselves if we do not meet them. We are so battered by these cruel self-imposed rules that we are absolutely paralyzed; taking action becomes impossible. Some procrastinators simply want to avoid the unpleasantness of doing something outside their nice, warm comfort zone. They would rather stay comfortable than

93

take the risk of moving into unknown territories. They prefer fantasy over reality. Still others will procrastinate because they are waiting to be inspired. They forget that sometimes you just have to take action first, instead of waiting to be sufficiently motivated. Inspiration is largely a luxury reserved for the amateur. Professionals can't afford to wait for inspiration or they would go broke. Furthermore, inspiration tends to favor those that make a daily commitment to their goals. The commitment comes first. The thrill of getting away with something or living on the edge can also trigger our procrastination. We might prefer the high of chaos to the peacefulness that comes when we meet our obligations in a timely fashion. Like a gambler at the casino, we gamble with time. Unfortunately, the majority of people at casinos go home broke! Lastly, some folks procrastinate because they want to avoid the responsibility associated with completing an action. It can be easier to tell others that we missed the deadline than letting them know we were rejected from a school or job we apply to. Avoidance and denial fester in 100 different forms, all robbing us of the joy and self-esteem that comes with taking action.

There are a few excellent tools that will help you with time management and procrastination. One is the practice of tracking your time. This way you can see exactly where it goes. It's like looking at your bank statement. It only works if you are honest, however! There are a few cell phone apps that do this for you, or you can create an Excel spreadsheet and simply write down each activity and how much time you spend on it. After a week or so, you can pinpoint exactly what activities are eating up the most of your disposal hours. If your time record shows 10 hours on Facebook, but you claim you don't have time to read a book, take a class or go hiking, you might be in for a rude awakening. Time tracking creates transparency, and once we know exactly how and where we waste time, it makes it harder to keep doing it. Eventually we have to take responsibility for our priorities in life. If watching 900 episodes of Law and Order is truly how you envisioned spending your summer, than stand behind that. But don't tell yourself you lack the time to write that novel!

Equal but opposite to the procrastinator is the person that must stay compulsively busy in order to feel worthwhile. Busyness can take the form of constantly engaging with technology, being a workaholic, or an obsession with productivity. While the busy bee may seem like they are on top of their game, they are really engaged in another form of avoidance, unable to abide stillness for self-reflection even for a moment. In our country it is not uncommon for workers to be at the office 60 or 70 hours, but all of this busyness comes at a steep price. It takes a heavy toll on our health, our relationship, our sanity. In order to maintain balance, we need vacations, breaks, siestas and downtime. Otherwise we cannot process the things we have learned or contemplate the goals we have yet to achieve. We're just rats on a wheel. To revisit the seed metaphor, there is always a gestation period before our plants bear fruit. Organic growth is a process that we cannot rush. It follows the arcs of the seasons and the planets, but sadly in our post-industrial society we are often sorely out of touch with the rhythms of nature. Instant gratification 24 hours a day keeps us enslaved to hyper-productivity. The point is, no matter how eager you are to reach your destination, it matters how you get there. What good will your success be if you are too exhausted, drained or distracted to really enjoy it? Try to savor the journey, taking small, practical steps every day towards your goals. As long as you don't stop moving in the right direction, you will arrive. Life is not a race!

In addition to being a manifestation of our internal beliefs about what we deserve and what we can contribute, prosperity and success in business is largely due to the quality of our work relationships. Cultivating mutually respectful, mutually-benefitting partnerships with bosses, clients and coworkers is a sure path to increasing our paychecks. It is more profitable to lock hands with people than to lock horns! We have to learn how to agree to disagree; how to cooperate with rather than compete with; how to distance ourselves from workplace gossip and other negativity; and how to disarm volatile people with peacefulness and humor. Too often we use the people we work with as canvasses onto which we project all the toxic damage from our family of origin. This transference causes us to sabotage these potential long-term partnerships.

There are some excellent tools for improving business relationships. One is to always practice the 24 hour rule. This means not responding to an upsetting text, email or phone call for a whole day so that we have time to cool off, gather our wits and proceed professionally. While it's so important to feel our feelings and express our emotions personally, in the workplace, self-restraint is a virtue. Always strive to keep things positive, because this becomes your professional reputation. How you treat people is a boomerang!

Above all, do not fear money. Money is neither inherently good nor bad. It is simply a form of energy. It affords us comfort, free time, ease, pleasure and increased opportunities for self-care and service to others. It's not a weapon to use against other people or against ourselves. It is simply a tool. Making the acquisition of material wealth one's sole goal in life is the same as pretending money doesn't exist and being a hobo. Both are rather lonely and sad ways to spend our time here on Earth. Remember that money and spirituality are not mutually exclusive. While some religions would have you believe that being poor is a virtue, the amount that you earn doesn't dictate your integrity or the contents of your heart. There are plenty of poor people that are cruel and corrupt, and there are plenty of rich people who are altruistic, pure and extremely generous. You can achieve happiness regardless of your present economic circumstances, but as your inner values and your outer behaviors move into greater and greater alignment, you will find you receive all that you ever needed or wanted. As you learn to respect time, work harmoniously with others and set aside your ego-based fears, you will come to know a prosperity you never thought possible. You will find that all along, the Universe was trying to lead you to abundance. You were just standing in your own way, blocking it out.

Like Dorothy in the Wizard of Oz, you had within you the power to create a beautiful, successful and miraculous life all along. May you tap that power now!

Conclusion

As you come to the end of this book, I want to congratulate you on completing this phase of your journey. You have proven to be your own hero, an individual of action. You have faced your demons, and conquered your fears. You have surrendered to love. Our healing and growing is never done, but by reading *Mental Detox* in its entirety, you have taken huge leaps and bounds towards self-mastery and self-awareness. There are many other aspects to living a life of abundance and joy that are not covered in this book, but these are yours to explore and incorporate as you discover them. Your garden now has a solid, sustainable foundation and you can add as many types of flowers, plants, fruit trees and ponds as you see fit. You are finally conscious of your own power and strength. You have truly taken ownership of your life. As by now you are fully familiar with the Law of Attraction, it will be easy to identify all the positive external blessings that come your way as the result of this intense internal work.

If you ever stumble, you can always return to the concepts in this book to regain your footing. Sometimes when things improve radically in our lives as the result of hard work and counseling, we can experience a kind of culture shock. We don't recognize or relate to our new selves. We are like a thin person that has lost 200 pounds, yet still sees an obese body when they look in the mirror.

We may have trouble trusting or believing that things have really changed, despite all the outward signs and confirmations. We may also feel self-conscious about our transformation. Is it safe for us to be this successful, beautiful and rich? This adjustment phase can be confusing, so remember that just because you have arrived at another level of consciousness, it doesn't mean you now have to go at things alone. You deserve to be supported and nurtured at every stage of your life, no matter how glorious your circumstances – not just when you are in pain or struggling. You deserve love and support *always* because you are human.

As always, I wish for you only the greatest love, the greatest success and the greatest freedom. It is also my sincere hope that you will take all you have learned and pass it on to others that you come into contact with. We are all connected, and when one of us finds peace and joy, we are all elevated. Enlightenment is contagious! There is an old children's story about a wall of caterpillars. Each was crawling and climbing on top of the next trying to reach the sky. This pillar of caterpillars stretched hundreds of feet into the air, but the creatures could never reach their goal by using one another as a ladder. They stepped on each other's heads, squashing one another's faces, but the more they competed for a higher position, the further down the totem pole they landed. One day, a beautiful butterfly with orange and blue wings flew up to the topmost caterpillar and taught him the secret of flight. He climbed the long journey down the pile and found a safe, beautiful tree in which he could build his cocoon. He missed his friends, but he knew he had to learn how to fly by going inwards. A long time passed as he matured and transformed. Then one day, he emerged, magnificent. He couldn't believe how easy it was now to achieve his goal and kiss the sky. He joined his butterfly mate and they soared the heavens. So you see, as you liberate yourself from the shackles of your past, your fears and your self-sabotaging behaviors, you unconsciously give all others the permission to do the same. You become a healer yourself.

Continued blessings until next time,

Cheyenne.

About the Author

Cheyenne Bryant is an experienced Life Coach. For years she has shared her wisdom, awareness, and insight through lectures, and assisting individuals with life impairments and challenges. For information about Life Coaching and lectures please contact DrBryant@Drbryant.co.

Made in the USA
Columbia, SC
27 August 2024

41257364R00069